Twayne's English Authors Series

EDITOR OF THIS VOLUME

Kinley Roby

Northeastern University

Kingsley Amis

TEAS 319

KINGSLEY AMIS

By PHILIP GARDNER

Memorial University of Newfoundland

TWAYNE PUBLISHERS
A DIVISION OF G. K. HALL & CO., BOSTON

Published in 1981 by Twayne Publishers,
A Division of G. K. Hall & Co.
All Rights Reserved

Printed on permanent/durable acid-free paper and bound
in the United States of America

First Printing

Library of Congress Cataloging in Publication Data

Gardner, Philip.
Kingsley Amis.

(Twayne's English authors series ; TEAS 319)
Bibliography: p. 166–71
Includes index.
1. Amis, Kingsley—Criticism and interpretation.
PR6001.M6Z67   828'.91409   80-22104
ISBN 0-8057-6809-2

Contents

About the Author
Preface
Chronology

1. Amis's Life 13
2. *Lucky Jim* (1954) 23
3. Amis the Moralist 37
4. The Amis Hero and "Abroad" 49
5. Amis's God 63
6. Alternate Worlds of Youth 77
7. "The Only End of Age" 92
8. "A Higher Art": Amis's Poetry 113
9. Other Fiction 132
10. An Interim Assessment 144
    Notes and References 153
    Selected Bibliography 166
    Index 172

About the Author

Philip Gardner was born in 1936 in Liverpool, England. He read English at King's College, Cambridge, and later obtained his Ph.D. from the University of Liverpool. After teaching for four years at universities in Japan, he took up in 1964 a post at the Memorial University of Newfoundland, where since 1975 he has been Professor of English.

Dr. Gardner has published two books of poetry, *The Deserted Vicarage* (1959) and *A View of the Island* (1970), and his articles on contemporary British and American poetry and fiction have appeared in scholarly journals in Canada, the United States, England, and Japan. He has published books on Norman Nicholson (Twayne, 1973) and E. M. Forster (Longman, 1977), and has edited *E. M. Forster: The Critical Heritage* (Routledge & Kegan Paul, 1973). He is also coauthor (with Averil Gardner) of *The God Approached: A Commentary on the Poems of William Empson* (Chatto & Windus, 1978).

Dr. Gardner is currently working on an annotated edition of E. M. Forster's *Commonplace Book*, to be published in England by the Scolar Press.

Preface

Ever since Lucky Jim Dixon rotated the affectations of scholars on the spit of his self-disgust—only partly comical—it has behoved them to think carefully before introducing any subject of discussion as a "strangely neglected topic." To introduce in such terms the work of Lucky Jim's creator, Kingsley Amis, may thus appear especially risky. And yet, though the face and personality of Amis are known to British television audiences (the word game "Call My Bluff"), readers of *Penthouse* ("Kingsley on Drink") and scanners of glossy magazine advertisements ("Very Kingsley Amis. Very Sanderson."), his novels and poetry—the gold bars, so to speak, that back up this paper currency—are indeed a topic "strangely neglected" by academic criticism. The best essay on his work remains, in my view, a chapter in David Lodge's *Language of Fiction*, published as long ago as 1966. There have been other essays, before and since, and there are fifteen perceptive pages in Bernard Bergonzi's *The Situation of the Novel* (1970); but although there are full-length books on some of Amis's contemporaries—Philip Larkin, Iris Murdoch, even John Braine—there is not yet one on Amis himself. This is a strange situation for a writer whose novels, particularly, have been so widely read since *Lucky Jim* appeared in 1954, and whose distinctive way with language—to speak of nothing else—has made it necessary to coin the epithet "Amisian," an epithet which, like "Pinteresque," acknowledges not just a personal style but the capturing in that style of a quality in life, and in human response to it, which had previously been sensed but "ne'er so well expressed."

A book on Amis seems therefore overdue, though this one cannot aim to be either comprehensive or final. Not comprehensive, because Amis is a man of letters rather than simply a writer, whose voluminous output embraces poetry, novels, short stories, essays, television plays, a study of Rudyard Kipling, the *New Oxford Book of Light Verse*, a survey of science fiction *(New Maps of Hell)*, a companion to James Bond studies, and a neo–James Bond novel, *Colonel Sun*, published under the pen-name Robert Markham; not to mention *On Drink* and Amis's trenchant contributions to the *Black Papers* on education in England. I shall devote most of the ensuing chapters to the large creative core of his work: his poetry, his short stories, and his thirteen novels to date (1979). But since Amis is still under sixty, and his rate of novel-production—a crude phrase but appropriate to the determined professionalism of Amis's outlook—has been about one novel every two years, my study cannot be final; nor am I so academic as to wish it to be.

Nevertheless, despite these necessary limitations, 1979 may well be a particularly suitable year in which to take stock of Amis's considerable achievement, and to chart his progress from the academe of the fairly innocent Jim Dixon to that of the experience-scarred Jake Richardson (1978). In 1979 Amis's *Collected Poems* were published, the volume spanning a period that began ten years before *Lucky Jim;* and in the *Observer* for April 1 of that year Amis humorously figured as one of four men "at the top of their careers" who had decided to "drop out." A carefully posed photograph, showing Amis seated beside his dog and his dog's dishes, gazing up in lotus position from the floor of his immaculate Hampstead kitchen, was accompanied by a statement that he was now so disgusted by "the way our society is degenerating" that he was opting out of it, and out of writing, in order "to develop my stunted spiritual faculties."

In view of the bleakness and irritation of much of Amis's writing in the last ten years, one's sense of the poetic truth of his "decision" is in no way reduced by the fact that its announcement was an April Fools' Day joke. Indeed, the feeling that Amis is sincerely pessimistic about the future of Western society, if not about writing, is only reinforced by Auberon Waugh's earlier news (given at the end of an interview with Amis published in the *Sunday Telegraph* of September 17, 1978) that Amis's next novel was to be set fifty years on, in a Britain taken over by Russia.

I am grateful to The Canada Council for awarding me a grant which enabled me to do research for this book in England; to the staffs of Memorial University Library and Cambridge University Library; to Professor James Kinsley and Mrs. Olwen Hackett (formerly Lady Brogan) for their reminiscences of Amis at Swansea and Cambridge; and to my wife and colleague, Averil Gardner, who as always has listened to my speculations and improved them with her own.

I am indebted to the author and to the following publishers for permission to quote from copyright material by Kingsley Amis: to Victor

Preface

Gollancz Ltd. and Doubleday & Co. Inc. for *Lucky Jim;* to Victor Gol-
lancz Ltd. and Jonathan Clowes Ltd.for *That Uncertain Feeling* and
I Like It Here; to Victor Gollancz Ltd. and Harcourt Brace Jovanovich
Inc. for *Take a Girl like You, One Fat Englishman, The Anti-Death
League;* to Jonathan Cape and Harcourt Brace Jovanovich Inc. for
What Became of Jane Austen? and *Other Questions, The Green
Man, Girl, 20, The Riverside Villas Murder, Ending Up;* to Jonathan
Cape and Viking Penguin Inc. for *The Alteration;* to Hutchinson Pub-
lishing Group and Viking Penguin Inc. for *Jake's Thing* and *Collected
Poems 1944-1979.*

For permission to quote from *On the Outskirts* by Michael Frayn,
I am indebted to the author, Collins Ltd. and Elaine Greene Ltd. For
permission to quote from *The Whitsun Weddings* by Philip Larkin,
I am indebted to the author and Faber and Faber Ltd. For permission
to quote from *Right Ho, Jeeves* by P. G. Wodehouse, I am indebted
to A. P. Watt, Ltd.

PHILIP GARDNER

Memorial University of Newfoundland

Chronology

1922   Kingsley William Amis born April 16 in a nursing home on the edge of Clapham Common, South London. Brought up in Norbury, London S.W.16. Early education at local schools.

1934–   Won scholarship to City of London School, a public school for
1941   day boys near Blackfriars Bridge, London.

1941–   Exhibitioner of St. John's College, Oxford. Read English
1942   Literature.

1942–   Army service, Royal Corps of Signals. Served in Normandy,
1945   Belgium, and Germany. Reached rank of lieutenant.

1945–   Completed education at Oxford. First-class degree in English (1947). Unsuccessful research for Oxford B. Litt. degree.

c.1949 Edited *Oxford Poetry 1949* with James Michie.

1947   *Bright November*, Amis's first volume of poetry, published by The Fortune Press.

1948   Married Hilary Ann Bardwell.

1949–   Lecturer in English, University College, Swansea.
1961

1953   *A Frame of Mind: 18 Poems.*

1954   *Lucky Jim* published in January. Poems by Amis published as Fantasy Press Pamphlet No. 22.

1955   *That Uncertain Feeling.* Won Somerset Maugham award for *Lucky Jim.*

1956   *A Case of Samples (Poems 1945–1956).*

1958   *I Like It Here. Lucky Jim* filmed (with Ian Carmichael, Terry-Thomas, Hugh Griffith, Sharon Acker).

1958–   Visiting Fellow in Creative Writing, Princeton University.
1959

1960   *Take a Girl like You. New Maps of Hell* (collection of Amis's lectures on science fiction, given at Princeton).

1961–   Fellow and Director of Studies in English, Peterhouse,
1963   Cambridge.

1962   *My Enemy's Enemy* (short stories). *That Uncertain Feeling* filmed (with Peter Sellers, Mai Zetterling, Virginia Maskell). *The Evans Country* (poems).

1963   *One Fat Englishman*. Gave up university teaching to concentrate entirely on writing.

1965   *The Egyptologists* (novel, in collaboration with Robert Conquest). Married Elizabeth Jane Howard.

1966   *The Anti-Death League*.

1967   *A Look Round the Estate (Poems 1957–1967)*.

1967-   Visiting Professor for one semester at Vanderbilt University,
1968   Nashville, Tennessee.

1968   *I Want It Now. Colonel Sun* (a James Bond novel, under the pseudonym Robert Markham).

1969   *The Green Man*.

1970   *What Became of Jane Austen? and Other Questions* (essays). *Take a Girl like You* filmed (with Hayley Mills and Oliver Reed).

1971   *Girl, 20*.

1972   *Dear Illusion* (short story).

1973   *The Riverside Villas Murder*.

1974   *Ending Up*.

1976   *The Alteration* (awarded the 1976 John W. Campbell Memorial Award for science fiction). Moved from large house ("Lemmons") on Hadley Common near Barnet to a smaller house in Flask Walk, Hampstead. October, made Honorary Fellow of St. John's College, Oxford.

1978   *Jake's Thing*.

1979   *Collected Poems 1944–1979*.

CHAPTER 1

Amis's Life

I Orientation

"NOTHING, like something, happens anywhere." So Philip Larkin, Amis's contemporary and friend, summed up his life as an only child in the Midlands city of Coventry.[1] Much the same offhand attitude has been displayed by Kingsley Amis himself, in a number of interviews he has given in the last decade, about his own early years. In 1975 he described the nursing home off Clapham Common in which he was born as "now, thankfully, demolished"; and the south London suburb, between Streatham and Croydon, in which he was brought up was "a place called Norbury—it had to be called something."[2] Yet his fiction and poetry tell a rather different, and warmer, story. Amis's first home in Norbury, 14 Buckingham Gardens, is not difficult to relate to "Montrose, alternatively 19 Riverside Villas" in *The Riverside Villas Murder* (1973); the novel is permeated by period nostalgia, and both the period and the place are those in which Amis grew up. Reg, the "particular friend" of its boy hero, Peter Furneaux, turns up as "Bobby Bailey" in a recent autobiographical poem of that title, and at the end of it Amis's regret for the loss of the past is conveyed as unequivocally as his predilection for the oblique allows:

I know

"The past" is a good name for what's all over;
    You can't, in fact, return
To what isn't a place. It does sound like an
    Easy lesson to learn.[3]

The contrast between Amis the private creator and Amis the public commentator, revealed here by his different views of Norbury, is an instructive one, and recommends the need for care in trying to sum up a writer in whom irony, satire, comedy, and indirection (what Donald

13

Davie has called "obliquities of provisional assent"[4]) vie with a wish to believe in, and to assert, quite straightforward and traditional notions of decent feeling and behavior. Amis the entertainer, Amis the debunker (guises in which, one feels, he has always been more acceptable to the common reader, and to many a reviewer and blurb-writer) is perpetually "surprising"—in Philip Larkin's words—"a hunger in himself to be more serious"[5]; and this has been so from the start. Likewise the Amis who admires, recommends, and practices invention— "fiction as fiction"[6]—is indebted like other writers to material derived from his own life.

II *Preparation*

Though not, in Amis's view, a "real place," Norbury, ten miles south of the River Thames and the City of London, was a pleasant and very respectable suburb, bisected by the small River Graveney. It had grown up around a station on one of the Southern Railway's lines from London to the south coast. Kingsley Amis's father, William Robert Amis, commuted daily into London on this railway; the son of a former glass-merchant, he was himself a senior clerk in the export department of Colman's Mustard, a lover of cricket and of Gilbert and Sullivan, and, by origin at least, a Baptist. He and his wife, Rosa, had met as fellow-members of the Congregation at the Baptist Chapel in Denmark Hill, some five miles nearer the center of London. Both later reacted against chapel-going, however, and their only child was thus brought up in the Protestant ethic of respectability and hard work, but without the Christian belief which had originally given rise to it. Such an atmosphere, a typically lower-middle-class one, tends to involve friction for any child of intellectual spirit, and Amis has described something of this, without rancor, in his essay "A Memoir of My Father" (1967).[7] In 1974, in the *Sunday Times*, he summed up his childhood as "very lonely. . . . I never had fun."

Nevertheless, Amis had both a doting, overprotective mother and a father who, for all his lowness of cultural brow, was ambitious that his son should succeed to an extent he felt he had not: money was stretched to provide Amis with the best education available. As a small boy at a local primary school, St. Hilda's, he fell in love with his English teacher, Miss Barr: to this event he later half-humorously ascribed his devotion to the glories of English literature.[8] At his next local school,

Norbury College, he fell in love with the headmaster's daughter and had published in the school magazine his earliest piece of fiction, a short adventure story entitled "The Sacred Rhino of Uganda." He also wrote there a ninety-nine-line poem, in blank verse, about the miracle of St. Sophia—a set subject, this, not a self-chosen one. Around 1933/1934, while at Norbury College, Amis discovered the world of popular fiction, popular music, films, and science fiction: a mass of "Yank Magazines" full of many-tentacled monsters in the local branch of Woolworth's.[9] Physical movement into a wider world also came in 1934, when Amis won a scholarship to the City of London School, an excellent public (i.e., private) school of 700 day boys overlooking the Thames by Blackfriars Bridge. Amis had become a commuter like his father, but of a different kind, and to a more fulfilling destination.

The initial fears of a twelve-year-old in this habitat of "self-possessed boys in black coats and striped trousers"[10] soon disappeared, and Amis's seven years at the City of London School seem to have been highly enjoyable. The teaching was of a very high standard, and the school itself heterogeneous in its intake, tolerant and without factions: a society which neither pressured its members to conform nor prompted the need to rebel. Within it Amis gained popularity by means of his gift for mimicry (so important a feature of his novels), but also became a sergeant in the school's Officer Training Corps. Mixing interest in world affairs with interest in the opposite sex, he joined the school branch of the League of Nations Union, which held its meetings jointly with the City of London School for Girls. He explored hobbies soon to be abandoned: painting in water-color, reading up on Dadaism and architecture. In the school magazine he published a long poem Eliot-esquely entitled "Prelude"; he later called it "a kind of suburbanite *Waste Land* tizzied up with bits of Wilde." When in the prewar summer of 1939 the school was evacuated to Wiltshire, to share the facilities of Marlborough College, Amis joined the chapel choir and found the experience of singing in four-part harmony "the apex . . . of non-sensual pleasures": a far cry from Lucky Jim, as was his ability to respond equally to Louis Armstrong and to a Mozart far from "filthy."

Sometime in 1940 Amis sat for a scholarship to St. Catharine's College, Cambridge. He failed to obtain it, but won instead an exhibition[11] to "one of the less pretentious Oxford Colleges,"[12] St. John's, where he started to read English in April 1941. His tutor was the Anglo-Saxon scholar Gavin Bone, who died in 1942. Amis respected his scholarship without—to judge from his dry poem "Beowulf"—being persuaded of the interestingness of Anglo-Saxon poetry:

> Someone has told us this man was a hero.
> But what have we to learn in following
> His tedious journey to his ancestors
> (An instance of Old English harking-back)?[13]

Already at St. John's when Amis came up was Philip Larkin. Their first encounter featured a display of Amis's histrionic ability and brilliant mimicry (Amis's "motor-bike-failing-to-start-noise" once convinced a motorcyclist that his machine was in serious trouble), and for the first time in his life Larkin felt himself "in the presence of a talent greater than my own."[14] The two became firm friends: *Lucky Jim* is dedicated to Larkin, and one of Larkin's poems in *The Less Deceived*, "Born Yesterday," is addressed to Amis's daughter Sally. Among other things Amis and Larkin shared an enthusiasm for jazz, the clarinettist and saxophonist "Pee Wee" Russell being, in Larkin's words, "our Swinburne and our Byron."

Unlike Larkin, however, who failed his army medical, Amis was liable for military service, and after one year at Oxford he was called up, in 1942. After Officer Training at Catterick Camp in North Yorkshire, he was commissioned in the Royal Corps of Signals, rising to the rank of lieutenant. Amis spent three and a half years in the army, the last fifteen months (though "none of it under fire"[15]) in Normandy, Belgium, and Germany. He did not enjoy much of this at the time, though it did not prevent his writing a good deal of poetry which appeared in his first volume, *Bright November* (1947). But he gained from his experience not only the material for three stories eventually collected in *My Enemy's Enemy* (1962) and, one must presume, the sense of male comradeship which forms the substructure of *The Anti-Death League*, but also, from a brother-officer in 1944, the quirk of pronunciation which issues in Bertrand Welch's "you sam." He had, when first at Oxford, briefly edited the University Labour Club Bulletin; but in a 1975 interview he credited his army experience with having stripped from him "a lot of callow left-wing ideas."[16] Nevertheless, in view of his continued, if ambivalent, expression of left-wing sympathies throughout the 1950s, one may surmise that the views of the young Lieutenant Archer, contemplating demobilization in the story "I Spy Strangers," are to some degree Amis's own. The postwar England Archer favors is "full of girls and drinks and jazz and books and decent houses and decent jobs and being your own boss."[17]

Amis came out of the army in 1945 and recorded his feelings in a longish poem entitled "Release," published in *Bright November* in 1947. It expresses fear and hope with a frank, lame vulnerability which is uncharacteristic of later Amis but very appealing. Whereas in 1965 Amis spoke bluffly of the army as having "lessened my fear of strangers," his twenty-years-earlier self listed some of its effects more dubiously:

> What have they [my dead comrades] given me?
> A catalogue of fears: of the telephone,
> Of entering a crowded room by myself,
> Of loud voices calling me to interview,
> Of typewritten notes, of arriving late at night
> Fearful they might have changed, fearful they cannot change.
> I have survived them too, and they have caused
> Nothing that will ever want to remember them.

Amis's long poem of the 1970s, "A Reunion," most recently gives the lie to this last claim, but even "Release" is full of the ambivalence wartime routine has caused: a wish to escape into "the days ahead," but a sense, too, that "here is danger from an obsessing dream." The poem concludes with a determination that points forward to the emergence of Amis the writer, in a world outside the absolving limitations of army life:

> Now I must awake and speak.
>   Now I must cause
> Something that will want to remember me.

III *Achievement*

In 1945 Amis returned to Oxford to complete his degree, and obtained First Class Honours in 1947. For his first year he overlapped with another budding writer, John Wain; the two "were united in homage to Larkin,"[18] and it was from Amis that John Wain bought his first copy of Philip Larkin's novel *Jill*, published in 1946. While at

Oxford, Amis also wrote a novel; entitled *The Legacy*, it remained unpublished, but later influenced Wain to begin his own first novel, *Hurry on Down*, which was published in 1953 and first introduced the "Angry Young Man" into British fiction. When, in the 1950s, Wain became editor of the BBC program "First Reading," he presented an episode from Amis's *Lucky Jim*. Thus one may see, in Oxford friendships of the 1940s, the partial beginnings of that shift from wartime romanticism which was to emerge in the 1950s as "the Movement."

Amis's own first appearance as a writer came in 1947, when a collection of thirty-one poems, most of them written after October 1943, was published under the title *Bright November* by The Fortune Press. Its proprietor, R. A. Caton, turns up in elusive Hitchcockian fashion in Amis's early novels as that "L. S. Caton" who is forever sending hastily torn-off notes in green ink which indicate that he will be writing again "before very long." But he was not, as Amis described him in 1974, a "vanity publisher,"[19] and his imprint was a prestigious one, since he had published Dylan Thomas's *18 Poems* in 1934 and identified some of the most promising talents of the 1940s: Philip Larkin's novel *Jill* and his first collection of poems, *The North Ship*, were both published by Caton. Little in *Bright November* comes up to the standard of these predecessors.

Between 1947 and 1949 Amis remained at Oxford as a research student, working on a B. Litt. thesis on the relationship between Victorian poetry and its reading public; he completed this but did not obtain the degree. He was also working on his novel *The Legacy* ("about a young man like myself, only nastier"[20]), and on a book about Graham Greene which had been commissioned, curiously, by an Argentinian university.[21] This, like the novel, was finished but not published; but its residual effect may be felt in *I Like It Here*, where Garnet Bowen updates his old notes on Graham Greene, and in *One Fat Englishman*, where Roger Micheldene, a bad Catholic, is described as having gone to school at Berkhamsted, as did Graham Greene, who was also born there.

Printed immediately before Amis's poem "Berkhamsted" in *Bright November* is his "Poem for Hilary." Amis married Hilary Ann Bardwell in 1948, and in 1949 he obtained a post in the English Department at the University College of Swansea, one of the four constituent colleges of the University of Wales. He found both Wales and Swansea congenial, and stayed there for twelve years. In 1954 James Kinsley, an Oxonian exactly one day younger than Amis, was appointed to the

Chair of English at Swansea; he describes Amis as having been "a loyal colleague and provocative teacher" and states that he was

a source of great fun in college society—an excellent mimic; and his action in building selected aspects of character and behaviour among his acquaintances into new characters showed itself at that time in *Lucky Jim* and *That Uncertain Feeling*.[22]

His Welsh experiences also led to some of Amis's most lively poems, his sequence "The Evans Country," and are reflected in his use of a Welsh background for the hero of *I Like It Here,* Garnet Bowen.

Lucky Jim was begun in 1951. The actual writing of it was made easier as a result of Amis's wife receiving a legacy of £2,000, with which they bought a house with a small study in the same district of Swansea, Uplands, in which Dylan Thomas had been born, in 1914. In the spring of 1951 Amis met Dylan Thomas when the latter gave a talk and a reading to the English Society of Swansea University College. Amis admired Dylan Thomas very much this side idolatry, and the evening was not in any case an unmixed success; but out of it came one item which was transferred into *Lucky Jim.* Dylan Thomas

announced, in his clear, slow, slightly haughty, cut-glass Welsh voice; "I've just come back from Persia, where I've been pouring water on troubled oil." Making what was in those days my stock retort to the prepared epigram, I said: "I say, I must go and write that down."[23]

Amis actually did, putting the phrase "their spectacular inability to pour water on troubled oil" into the mouth of Bertrand Welch in Chapter 4. Its context, the madrigal-singing weekend at the Welch's house, was derived from the proclivities of Amis's parents-in-law, who were keen practitioners of folk-dancing; the substitution of madrigals for this form of "arty" culture was tactful, but caused Amis "agony."[24]

In 1953 a small collection of Amis's poems, *A Frame of Mind,* was published in a limited edition by the University of Reading School of Art. The collection, which included such characteristic satirical pieces as "A Dream of Fair Women" and "Something Nasty in the Bookshop,"[25] was dedicated appropriately to John Wain, now a Lecturer in English at Reading, whose own slim volume *Mixed Feelings* had in 1951 inaugurated this local venture into small-scale publishing. *A Frame of Mind* marked Amis's appearance as a recognizably individ-

ual poet, despite the strong overlay of Robert Graves which had begun
to replace the Auden influence detectable throughout *Bright November;* it was favorably received, but in terms which, in view of Amis's
too thoroughgoing later reputation as an iconoclast, it is now salutary
to recall: "a sensitive reader . . . will detect the modesty and good feeling that underlie Mr. Amis's 'toughness.'"[26]

All these qualities were also recognized when *Lucky Jim* (completed
at the end of 1952) was published by the left-wing firm of Gollancz in
January 1954, establishing Amis's existence with the general public as
A Frame of Mind had established it with the intelligentsia the previous
year. Whatever the misreadings of *Lucky Jim* which caused it to be
seen as a novel of ideological revolt against an upper-middle-class
"Establishment," whatever the oversimplifying influence of the changing climate of literature and society in the mid-1950s, *Lucky Jim*
undoubtedly possessed qualities which caused it to appeal to both critics and public in large measure: its comedy of situation, its catchy tricks
with language, its element of wish-fulfillment, its sympathetic hero.
The book went through ten impressions in 1954, four in 1955, three
apiece in 1956 and 1957; in 1958 it was filmed; and recently its sales
were reportedly proceeding at a steady 50,000 a year. This fame has
been, in literary terms, something of a drawback; later books by Amis
have sometimes been seen as falling off in comedy rather than increasing in seriousness. And this very formulation is itself based on a view
of Amis which overemphasizes his satirical and "rebellious" elements;
many of his later novels are more justly appreciated if one agrees to
recognize much in *Lucky Jim* which is not "funny" but simply a serious and interesting treatment of a credible situation. Though at the
end of the novel Jim Dixon is indeed "lucky" (and, during it, ironically
lucky), *Lucky Jim* as a title is a touch flippant, suggesting that events
take place in a comic postcard world rather than a real one. To invoke
the name of E. M. Forster in connection with Amis may seem strange,
but Amis does to some extent share with Forster a mixed method of
presentation, a tendency to undercut the serious with the irreverent
which may make it difficult to know how to take him. One recalls Lionel Trilling's witty summary of the Forsterian manner: "'Wash ye,
make yourselves clean—if you can find the soap.'"[27]

W. Somerset Maugham—senior, "establishment," expatriate—
referred to the British "Angry Young Men" of the mid-1950s as
"scum."[28] Insofar as Amis, as a result of *Lucky Jim*, was classified with
them, it is ironical that, also as a result of *Lucky Jim*, he should have

won the Somerset Maugham award. This carried with it the condition that the winner spend some time abroad. Curiously for an allegedly left-wing writer, Amis chose to visit (in 1955, the year his second novel, *That Uncertain Feeling,* appeared) the Portugal of Dr. Salazar. Out of this came his third novel, *I Like It Here,* which is among other things an amusing study of British, or Amisian, xenophobia, and perhaps his most lighthearted and most easily enjoyable book.[29] Another trip abroad came in 1958–59, when Amis spent a year as Creative Writing Fellow at Princeton University. There he gave a semester's worth of lectures, as part of the Christian Gauss Seminars in Criticism, on the unusual subject of Science Fiction, later turning his lectures into the book *New Maps of Hell.* He also used his experiences while at Princeton as the basis for *One Fat Englishman* (1963); he himself, like Roger Micheldene, had the script of one of his lectures stolen, though after the lecture, not before it. A further visit to America came in 1967, when he spent a semester as Visiting Professor at Vanderbilt University, Tennessee, the alma mater of John Crowe Ransom; this visit enabled him to write his bleak poem about racism, "South," and, in terms of local color, was reflected in the "Fort Charles" section of *I Want It Now* (1968).

In 1961 Amis resigned his post at Swansea to become Fellow and Director of Studies in English at Peterhouse, Cambridge. The poet and critic Donald Davie, a contemporary himself lecturing at Cambridge then, has described Amis's time there as a "brief but eventful and unhappy period"; in Davie's view, a writer like Amis, with his serio-comic manner, did not fit easily into the distrustful and entirely "serious" atmosphere of Cambridge. Indeed, F. R. Leavis, annoyed by his appointment, described Amis at a faculty meeting as no more than a "pornographer."[30] Amis's disappointment with Cambridge is adequately presented in his essay "No More Parades" (1964), but one of his reasons is adumbrated by a passage at the beginning of *Lucky Jim* which describes Jim and Professor Welch in conversation, from the point of view of a possible onlooker:

He and Welch might well be talking about history, and in the way history might be talked about in Oxford and Cambridge quadrangles. At moments like this Dixon came near to wishing that they really were.

The discussion of English Literature at Cambridge proved, in the event, not to live up to such expectations. But one incident from Amis's

Cambridge period is worth recording, since it retrospectively validates
the farcical scene in *That Uncertain Feeling* (Ch.10) in which John
Lewis escapes from the Gruffydd-Williamses' house dressed as a Welsh
woman in national costume. An eye-witness has described a party held
in Jesus College:

The party was just getting going in its dignified way when in came two
remarkable looking ladies who caught all eyes. As the dust settled it became
apparent that they looked more like pantomime dames than anything
else. . . . They certainly brightened up the proceedings.[31]

Both "ladies" were men; one of them was Kingsley Amis.

Amis left Cambridge, and academic life, in 1963, and became a full-
time professional writer. For a while he contemplated settling in
Majorca (as Robert Graves had done), but instead met, and in 1965
married,[32] the novelist Elizabeth Jane Howard. Since then his life, first
in a large, nine-bedroom house at Hadley Common in Hertfordshire,
now in the well-to-do but artistic London suburb of Hampstead, has
been that of an affluent, hard-working author whose hostility to the
social and cultural "Establishment," insofar as it was ever strong, has
given way to a typically English conservatism, more eager to remember than to look forward, more eager to preserve than to debunk.
"Writers," Amis has recently said, "should notice that their great predecessors have always sooner or later come down on the side of tradition."[33] And the laughter has grown more harsh, the contemplating eye
more somber, as the enemies of life have revealed themselves to be less
insincerity, affectation, the crypto-Fascist, and the "trendy Lefty,"
than the decline of desire, the emptiness of old age, and death. What
remains to be faced, and how, is stated with old-soldier dignity at the
end of "A Reunion," first published in 1977:

> Disbandment has come to us
> As it comes to all who grow old;
> Demobilised now, we face
> What we faced when we first enrolled.
> Stand still in the middle rank!
> See you show them a touch of pride!—
> Left-right, left-right, bags of swank—
> On the one-man pass-out parade.[34]

CHAPTER 2

Lucky Jim *(1954)*

THE 1950s in England were, for younger writers, a period of reaction against the literary attitudes of the 1930s and 1940s. This reaction is documented in Chapter 8, in which I deal with Amis's career as a poet. But the period was also, for younger people in general, one of gradual social change, of dissatisfaction with the hegemony of middle-class values and culture, and of irritation at the exclusive hold on the best jobs apparently maintained by the products of the public schools and the old universities of Oxford and Cambridge. The latter group were labeled "the Establishment"; their opponents, on the appearance in 1956 of John Osborne's play *Look Back in Anger*, were given by journalism the now well-known title "Angry Young Men." Such labels may now be thought simplistic conveniences, but they were convenient because they did label something: a widespread sense that society needed to be changed, or at least modified. Ironically, this sense of dissatisfaction was one of the results of the very machinery which had been designed to broaden the availability of life's advantages: the Education Act of 1944.

Before World War II a free elementary education up to the age of fourteen was guaranteed by the state. Access to secondary education, however, was very largely restricted to those who could afford to pay for it; though some assistance was provided in the form of scholarships, a considerable financial burden fell on the parents of the comparatively few working-class children to whom they were available. It is thus true to say that university education was almost exclusively a privilege enjoyed by the middle and upper-classes, and that its ethos was determined by their values. The Education Act of 1944 was intended to remedy this exclusiveness. It raised the minimum school-leaving age to fifteen and instituted a two-tier system of free secondary education consisting of "Grammar Schools" and "Secondary Modern Schools";

which type a child entered was determined by an examination taken at the age of eleven or thereabouts—the "eleven-plus" examination. Those who passed entered grammar school and, after a further set of hurdles, became eligible for a liberally state-assisted education at university.

The good intentions of this Utopian scheme, put into operation by the Labour government elected at the end of the war, are hardly to be faulted: to educate each person "according to his age, aptitude and ability." Their effects, however, were perhaps too far-reaching, and it is important to realize the degree of hostility with which Kingsley Amis, himself a beneficiary of the prewar system, has reacted to the ultimate development of the postwar one, in the 1960s: the foundation of the "New" universities and the rise of the Comprehensive School. In the 1950s, the Education Act did achieve its aim of broadening the university intake to include more working-class students, intending them to assimilate, and be assimilated by, the culture of the higher classes by whom the universities had been dominated; but the process—since the attitudes of society change less quickly than administrative fiats might wish—gave rise to a significant number of deracinated and disoriented young men, no longer at home in their working- or lower-middle-class attitudes and environments, but at the same time not feeling accepted by the social system into which their education appeared to be pushing them. The reaction to this phenomenon—uncertainty, resentment, envy[1]—could express itself in four basic ways: an attempt to "opt out" (which is made, for instance, by John Wain's hero Charles Lumley in *Hurry on Down*); an attempt to find a congenial niche in that world (which is roughly the course of Amis's Jim Dixon); an attempt to conquer that world by its own methods, perhaps doing violence to part of one's nature in the process (which happens to John Braine's nonuniversity Joe Lampton in *Room at the Top*); and, eventually, an attempt to change social patterns so that working-class attitudes and the possession of a university degree would no longer appear incompatible.

It is the kind of society this has in part produced, that of the late 1960s and the 1970s, to which Kingsley Amis has latterly voiced his objections;[2] but it was against the more indecisive stirrings of the 1950s that he first emerged as a novelist, and in the context of these his first novel, *Lucky Jim*, had a topical meaning—to some extent imported into it—which cannot be fully appreciated without the preliminary survey that I have attempted, however summarily, to provide here.

I *Author, Character, and Story*

The origin of *Lucky Jim* was a visit Amis paid in 1946 to his friend
Philip Larkin, then an assistant librarian at University College, Leicester.[3] Over coffee in the Common Room, it occurred to Amis that the
world of the provincial university was "totally uncharted territory,"
just waiting to be written about. One must presume that his own experience as a university assistant lecturer at Swansea, from 1949, crystal-
ized wish into performance. Amis has denied a close similarity between
the unnamed university college of *Lucky Jim* and those that begat and
nourished the novel; there is in it, he has said, "very little of Swansea
. . . and virtually nothing of Leicester."[4] Both these places, indeed,
seem to be deliberately mentioned in the novel in order that the reader
shall exclude them from it: "Abertawe" (Swansea stands on the River
Tawe) is where Professor Welch's friend Athro Haines teaches, and
Leicester is where Jim Dixon has taken his degree. Nevertheless, it can
hardly be fortuitous that Dixon's college is located opposite a cemetery,
as is Leicester University; and the townscape described at the end of
Chapter 3, clustering downhill around "a tapering cathedral spire," fits
Leicester better than anywhere.[5]

A more important consideration is the extent to which Jim Dixon
can be presumed to be Amis. Though it seems inherently unlikely that
the writer of a first novel will go to the trouble of creating a protagonist
utterly unlike himself, it is important to establish the degree of iden-
tification involved, since the literary folklore of the 1950s was quick to
blur author and hero into one, presuming not only that Jim Dixon was
a rebel but that Amis was a philistine. Clarity has hardly been assisted
by such a public statement of Amis's as his essay entitled "Why Lucky
Jim Turned Right," which expresses his own shift of political
sympathies.[6]

In many externals, at least, Jim Dixon is not Amis. Dixon comes from
the northwest of England[7] and has taken his degree at Leicester rather
than Oxford: in fact, he beats an Oxford candidate at his job interview.
Unlike Amis, he dislikes part-singing and classical music; like him,
however, he has a lower-middle-class background: Amis has recently
stated that he envisaged Dixon's father to have been "a small shop-
keeper, or a man in some commercial firm"[8]—as his own father was.
Dixon's military career, as "an RAF corporal in western Scotland,"
does not resemble that of Amis who, like Dixon's student Michie, was
an officer; nevertheless, Amis's officership was less active and glorious

than that of Michie, tank troop commander at Anzio, moustached and impeccably turned out. Here, Amis himself seems midway between the two characters. The most obvious difference between Amis and Dixon, of course, is the length of their respective academic careers, so that one cannot imagine the writer experiencing quite the same difficulties of adjustment as his character; but as Dixon fails to fit into his job, Amis failed to obtain his research degree at Oxford, and the scathing attention which Dixon devotes to the "niggling mindlessness" of his "Shipbuilding Techniques" article in Chapter 1 may express a vicarious revenge by Amis himself on his B. Litt. thesis, with its own generically similar title: "English Non-Dramatic Poetry, 1850–1900, and the Victorian Reading Public."

The dedication of *Lucky Jim* to Philip Larkin, reasonable in any case in view of the novel's origin, prompts one to wonder whether in one aspect at least Jim Dixon is a friendly skit on him. The contrast between Jim's highly verbalized relationship with Margaret Peel— "small, thin, bespectacled" (Ch. 2)—and his choked, intenser response to the beautiful Christine Callaghan has distinct affinities with the predicament, roughly contemporaneous with the novel, presented by Larkin in his poem "Wild Oats,"[9] with its frustrating opposition of a "bosomy English rose" and "her friend in specs I could talk to."

But whatever there may be in this possibility, and despite the distancing effect created by those elements in Dixon which are demonstrably not shared by Amis, one must concede a basic current of sympathy between them. Despite the use of a third-person mode of narration, what is narrated is seen almost entirely from Dixon's point of view. From the start one is drawn to identify with him, and only by deliberately forcing oneself to stand back (rarely does one seem invited to do this by the novelist) can one see the action, and the other characters, in terms other than his—terms, for instance, which would show Professor Welch and his son Bertrand as other than the "bad," as well as "ridiculous," persons Amis has recently claimed them to be.[10] Thus there is an element of "slanting" in the way the novel deals with its realistic milieu, its elements of farce and of fantasy being part of its slant.

Where there might be some danger of the reader's looking askance at Dixon's actions, as, for instance, in his theft of the Barclays' taxi and his final dropping of Margaret, compunction is diluted, or removed, by in the one case Dixon's own (passing) feeling of guilt, and in the other by Catchpole's revelations in Chapter 24 of the exhibitionistic aspect of Margaret's "attempted suicide." And though it is overdoing things to make Dixon out to be a Socialist ideologue, his egalitarian instincts revealed in Chapter 4, in the argument with Bertrand over the distribution of "buns," belong with the fuzzily expressed left-wing sympathies evident in Amis's Fabian Society pamphlet of 1957, *Socialism and the Intellectuals*. One may sum up by suggesting that, if Dixon isn't quite Amis, he is what Amis might have been had he not experienced public school, Oxford and an army commission, and that Dixon's actions and attitudes express in an exaggerated form the residual suspicion, eclecticism, and social unease which have persisted in Amis despite these smoothing experiences.

Lucky Jim inaugurates an authorial preference found in nine out of Amis's thirteen novels: it plunges straight *in medias res* with a conversation, leaving the reader to discover gradually where he is while he shares the experience and point of view of the protagonist, who is already there. But if the opening of *Lucky Jim* leaves the reader wondering where he is physically, it also shows its hero, Jim Dixon, a probationary assistant lecturer in his mid-twenties at a provincial university college, wondering where he is existentially: the questions for him may be expressed as "What I am doing here?", "Do I want to be here?", and "Is there anything I can do about it?" His situation, in fact, is his predicament, and the novel's twenty-five chapters, which cover the last four or five weeks in the summer of his first academic year, show his seriocomic attempts to deal with it, and his final escape from it by a combination of luck and personality.

Dixon's predicament is two-fold, academic and personal, and is presented in Chapters 1 and 2 in terms of the two people who embody it: his professor, "Neddy" Welch, infuriatingly vague and evasive, who may or may not recommend that Dixon be kept on for a second probationary year, and his slightly younger, though senior colleague, Margaret Peel, neurotic and of only "minimal prettiness" (Ch. 10), with whom largely by accident he has become entangled, and whose recent attempt at suicide he feels unnecessarily responsible for. What holds Dixon to Margaret is partly a likable kindness and concern, partly a fatalistic sense that better-looking girls are not for him, and one is both sympathetic about his problem and irritated by his lack of ruthlessness in cutting free of it. What holds him to Professor Welch—a devastating portrait, incidentally, of a certain type of British academic—is simpler: the desire to improve his chances of remaining in the History Department, by such proper but detested means as publication and his appar-

ently pleased acceptance of opportunities like giving a public lecture
on the vapid topic of his professor's choice: "Merrie England." Other
methods are even more repugnant to Jim, involving in his view "some
loss of time and integrity" (Ch. 17): indexing the notes for Welch's
book, spending seven hours looking up references for a lecture Welch
is to give, "remaining present and conscious while Welch talked about
concerts" (Ch. 1), and going to the "arty weekend" at Welch's house.

This, presented in all its excruciating, embarrassment-causing detail
in Chapters 4 through 7, has the reader largely on Dixon's side; the
references to P. Racine Fricker—the rebarbative, "coming composer"
of the early 1950s—the Anouilh play, and (in Ch. 1) to "a friend of
Peter Warlock's" are meant to pile on the agony of a milieu not simply
cultured, but strained and affected in its culture. Some of Dixon's
actions, however—walking out abruptly, getting drunk, making a
drunken pass at Margaret, burning the bedclothes—only command a
limited sympathy and highlight the false position he is in. The job he
wishes to keep is not one he enjoys, and it entails the ability—which
he does not possess—to function in an atmosphere he finds uncongenial. But one would not automatically agree that Dixon's inability to
sightread "Now is the Month of Maying" makes Thomas Morley a
worthless composer or those who enjoy him a pack of "pseuds."

Dixon's "faces"—such as his "shot-in-the-back face" made on being
approached by the unnervingly keen Michie (Ch. 3)—are all, as is
admitted in Chapter 25, "designed to express rage or loathing"; they
provide Dixon with release in a situation with which, until Christine
provides his vague aspirations with a human focus, he cannot deal
directly. Though they are very funny—like his "ape-imitation" on finishing writing his lecture (Ch. 20), and his fantasy of stuffing Welch
down the lavatory (Ch. 1)—they are not merely farcical: indeed, the
care for circumstantial detail in the "taxi-stealing" scene (Ch. 13)
seems almost designed to demonstrate that *Lucky Jim* is a realistic
novel. If Jim's uncertainties get him into amusing scrapes, they are not
the product of incompetence but of lack of confidence: he can do his
job but he does not believe in himself. Though, in Chapter 1, his professional policy is indicated as "to read as little as possible of any given
book," this seems more intended to explain his contretemps with
Welch over the book on enclosures than to be a general statement.
Elsewhere, there is evidence that he does work. He fails to see Margaret on the night of her attempted suicide because he is preparing a
lecture; the "checking" he does for Welch is "really splendid" (Ch. 18);
the problem with his public lecture is its mode of delivery, not—except

at the end—its content; what puts Miss McCorquodale, Miss O'Shaughnessy, and Miss ap Rhys Williams[11] off his special subject is the size of its reading list, not any inherent absurdity; when Dixon indicates to Michie that he can't "pronounce on the learned Scotus or Aquinas" (Ch. 3), his examples of scholasticism are correct, and there is no need for his worry "or should it have been Augustine?"; and, finally, the very fact that L. S. Caton steals Dixon's article and publishes it as his own may be taken as proof that Dixon can, if he wishes, produce the "right stuff."

But he does not, and as the novel progresses its essential subject changes from being a satire on university life and the provincial culture, tinged with snobbery, represented by the Welches and becomes Jim's search for, or at least movement toward, self-realization and self-fulfillment. Some of the virtues which have tied him to Margaret— "politeness, friendly interest, ordinary concern"—combine with a new but credible, if intermittent, decisiveness sparked by love, to rescue him from his previous life. As his problems, Welch and Margaret, are related, so are their solutions, in the persons of the beautiful Christine, a slightly blurred but delightful specimen of "nice," healthy 1950s girlhood, and her uncle Julius Gore-Urquhart, the rich patron of the arts who is also, as Amis has chosen recently to describe him, "a man of the people who has made his way."[12] The solution which comes through them—getting both the girl and the job coveted by the odious but not totally ridiculous Bertrand Welch—involves leaving the provinces for London, and fulfills, in an aesthetically satisfying fashion which counterbalances its touch of fairy-tale unlikeliness, the yearning vision which is described at the end of Chapter 2. This passage, the most lyrical in the entire novel, deserves to be quoted, since it hints, along with the few simple images of rural beauty elsewhere,[13] at an element in Amis which he all too seldom exposes:

As he stood in the badly-lit jakes, he was visited again, and unbearably, by the visual image that had haunted him ever since he took on this job. He seemed to be looking from a darkened room across a deserted back street to where, against a dimly-glowing evening sky, a line of chimney-pots stood out as if carved from tin. A small double cloud moved from right to left. The image wasn't purely visual, because he had a feeling that some soft unidentifiable noise was in his ears, and he felt with a dreamer's baseless conviction that somebody was going to come into the room where he seemed to be, somebody he knew in the image but not in reality. He was certain it was an image of London, and just as certain that it wasn't of any part of London he'd ever visited.

The center of the novel, the point at which the general shift in Dixon's fortunes toward "reassurance and hope" (Ch. 13) begins to be felt, is Chapters 10 through 15, which describe in great detail—Amis is very much a novelist of detail, both of fact and feeling—the college's Summer Ball and its aftermath. At it Dixon meets Gore-Urquhart, whose brisk, pleasant manner and "strong Lowland-Scottish accent" are nicely poised against his wealth and upper-class-sounding hyphenated name, and Dixon's "naïve" naturalness in the sharply observed scene over the "pints" (Ch. 10), is in marked contrast to the combination of obsequiousness and false familiarity displayed by Bertrand Welch and Margaret. Rapport between the two is clearly established, though, realistically, it is not dwelt on. Of more immediate concern to Dixon is the extension of his relationship with Christine, already established by her willingness to help over the burnt bedclothes (Ch. 6) and by the vein of childish irresponsibility then displayed by her, in welcome contrast to the "dignant" prissiness she has seemed to show in company.

The new masterfulness which Dixon displays in the Summer Ball sequence is given credibility by two things: his reaffirmed view that Christine is the girl he wants, and her appearance of being a "damsel in distress" (Bertrand is neglecting her); and by the encouragement he receives from Carol Goldsmith, the attractive wife of a colleague in the History Department, to make a move. The result of this advice is that Dixon and Christine leave the party and return to the Welch's house in a taxi, enterprisingly stolen from Barclay, the Professor of Music. Nevertheless, the tête-à-tête with Christine is worth it, proving to Dixon that "nice things are nicer than nasty ones" (Ch. 14)—a philosophy apparently simple but not always easy to put into practice, as Dixon discovers in Chapter 16 when Margaret's bout of hysterics, and her honesty and self-reproach, bring a return of his guilt, and the compunctious sense that "somewhere his path to Christine was blocked." Meanwhile, however, alone in the Welch's house, in a chapter (15) which skillfully mixes tenderness and friendly familiarity, Dixon and Christine have had their first kiss, and their obvious compatibility gives promise of a satisfactory conclusion.

The latter part of the novel, reasserting social pressures, Dixon's uncertainty about his professional future, and Christine's rather muddled sense of obligation to Bertrand, recalls the obstacles placed in the way of his two lovers by E. M. Forster in Part II of *A Room with a View*. One of the obstacles is the undue proprietorialness of Bertrand, who challenges Dixon to a fight and is knocked down; the fight is funny, but kept realistic by the small number of blows dealt and by the look of "embarrassed recognition" (Ch. 20) which the dazed Bertrand gives Dixon from the floor. Just as the Summer Ball sequence has led Dixon to realize openly what he wants and try for it, so this incident crystalizes verbally the coincidence in him of inner thought and outward behavior, previously kept frustratingly apart. David Lodge has rightly indicated as a turning-point, presented ritualistically by Amis, Jim's words to the prone Bertrand:

The bloody old towser-faced boot-faced totem-pole on a crap reservation, Dixon thought. "You bloody old towser-faced boot-faced totem-pole on a crap reservation," he said.[14]

It is also significant that when Michie enters at this point, Dixon is quite unembarrassed, speaks to him "smoothly," and copes amiably with the unwelcome news that Michie will be the only student taking his special subject next term—if there is one for Dixon.

Lucky Jim, which in its final chapters surges forward with the large, rhythmic authority of a symphony, can be said to have both a climax and a coda. The climax, fortissimo, is the "Merrie England" lecture (Ch. 22), which ends Dixon's professional career in a pyrotechnic display, fueled by alcohol and despair, of savage, unintended mimicry, bravura speed-reading, and a truncated but clear enough denunciation of the "arty" crowd whom he has felt obliged to please. Nothing, one may feel, becomes Dixon's academic life like his leaving it, and, curiously enough (but not really curiously), once matters are decided, he no longer resents Welch and feels "almost free of care" (Ch. 23). Whatever is to come, Dixon is no longer encumbered by falsities as much his own as belonging to others.

The coda, after his clarifying interview with Catchpole which frees him forever from his sense of responsibility for Margaret, is his bus journey to meet Christine, similarly freed by Carol Goldsmith from her loyalty to Bertrand. One notes in both cases the operation of a severe and perhaps oversimple morality: people who two-time (Bertrand with Carol, Margaret by trying to involve two men in her "suicide") can be discarded. But reservations about this mechanism of plot are swamped by the brilliantly hyperbolical description—surely one of the best passages of comic writing in English literature—of the bus journey, a slow-motion odyssey which keeps the reader, like Dixon, on the edge of his seat, biting his nails with tension, and in despair that such a lethargic bus—

Learners practised reversing across his path; gossiping knots of loungers parted leisurely at the touch of his reluctant bonnet; toddlers reeled to retrieve toys from under his just revolving wheels. (Ch. 24)

—will ever reach the station in time.

It misses the train, but not the girl, and as he and Christine are finally united, Dixon's urge to denounce the Welches, father and son, standing on the pavement, dissolves "in a howl of laughter" (Ch. 25). What once filled Dixon's horizon shrinks in significance and vanishes over it, as he and Christine walk away into their own lives with a final phrase that is simple description but also symbolic of the self-discovery—knowing what you are and being honest about what you want—which is the deepest theme of the novel:[15]

The whinnying and clanging of Welch's self-starter began behind them, growing fainter and fainter as they walked on until it was altogether overlaid by the other noises of the town and by their own voices.

II   *Style and Affinities*

There can be no doubt that *Lucky Jim* is an extraordinarily talented novel, rich in closely observed incident and in sharp depiction of character. Though I have deliberately emphasized its serious aspects, one of its talents is a formidable talent to amuse. Part of the humor is situational: Professor Welch pushing the revolving doors of the college library in the wrong direction (Ch. 17), the manic despair of Dixon's telephone conversation, as "Forteskyaw," with Mrs. Welch (Ch. 19). But a larger part of its humor is linguistic, involving jokes about speech-forms themselves, and particularly exploiting the absurd possibilities inherent in the literal interpretation of clichés.

To some degree these verbal tricks are reflections in language-terms of Dixon's own uncertainties about his position: for instance the sentence in Chapter 1 describing a voice singing above Dixon's head: "it sounded like, and presumably might even be, Barclay, the Professor of Music." But their continuation in almost all of Amis's novels makes it clear that they are a quirk, or predisposition, of Amis himself, who is prone, almost in the manner of an Oxford linguistic philosopher, to question the nature, and highlight the oddness, of phrases we use without thinking. After reading Amis, however, we are unlikely to do this again. There are too many examples to quote, but the first example in *Lucky Jim* is precisely identifiable, and occurs as a rude internal comment by Dixon on the ramblings of his professor:

"The young fellow playing the viola had the misfortune to turn over two pages at once, and the resulting confusion . . . my word. . . . "
   Quickly deciding on his own word, Dixon said it to himself and then tried to flail his features into some sort of response to humour. (Ch. 1)

Exactly the same pattern—an inner release mechanism—recurs when Christine is talking to Dixon about Bertrand in Chapter 14:

"He's such a queer mixture, you see."
   Naming to himself the two substances of which he personally thought Bertrand a mixture, Dixon said: "In what way?"

Another characteristic of language humor is Amis's establishment (in Ch. 4) of Bertrand's affected pronunciation "you sam" for "you see," a formula extended later into "obviouslam," "hostelram," and even "bam."[16] It is Dixon's rage with Bertrand's later utterance of "you sam" (Ch. 20) that crystalizes his detestation of Bertrand's fake artiness and inspires him to fight.
   Such self-conscious devices of language remind one that Amis is an academic, intellectual writer who is of the milieu which he presents. He is also a literary writer, and expects a reader who can pick up his references, as for instance when Dixon pulls his "Edith Sitwell face" (Ch. 9) and when, at the very end, Welch and Bertrand are reduced to caricatures by being described as "Gide and Lytton Strachey, represented in waxwork form by a prentice hand." Aristotle and I. A. Richards are debunkingly mentioned in Chapter 10. Less obvious is the reference to Graham Greene in Chapter 18: "He remembered a character in a modern novel Beesley had lent him who was always feeling pity moving in him like sickness, or some such jargon." It is typical of Amis, not just of Dixon's personally jaundiced view of literature, that this reference, intended to apply seriously to Dixon's state of mind, is presented as a skit: it is a way of making a necessary point without committing Amis to acceptance of the manner of the author

borrowed, and frequent instances in Amis of the habit lead one less to praise his wariness of affectation in others than to criticize his fear of open emotional statements by himself. Such self-protection—one of the less admirable characteristics of 1950s writing—takes the form also of private jokes: the introduction of "L. S. Caton," who is to recur in four more novels, and the use for Dixon's ex-officer student of the name "Michie," that of an undergraduate friend five years younger than Amis, but contemporary with him at Oxford, James Michie, who was a pacifist;[17] as, oddly enough, is Bertrand.

Walter Allen's proclamation, reviewing *Lucky Jim* in the *New Statesman*, that "a new hero has risen among us,"[18] places the novel in the context of the 1950s, alongside such novels as William Cooper's *The Struggles of Albert Woods* (1952), whose hero is also lower middle class, round-faced, short in stature, and "an excellent mimic." Its closest external resemblances, though, are to John Wain's *Hurry on Down* (1953), which Allen mentions. Some of these similarities are so close as to suggest that Amis and Wain showed each other their work in progress.[19] Both their titles are quoted from "Old Songs," and both have epigraphs announcing the fact;[20] Dixon and Wain's hero, Charles Lumley, are both History graduates; both heroes employ a kind of farcical ingenuity at moments of crisis; both are shown drinking in "Oak Lounges"; both, at the beginning, are shown as people who seethe inwardly with irritation and outrage, but speak mildly; both fall for their respective girls, Christine and Veronica, in a *coup de foudre;* and the type of quarreling, involving political as well as personal hostility, which occurs between Charles Lumley and Burge (*Hurry on Down*, Ch. 8) distinctly resembles that between Dixon and Bertrand.

Nevertheless, though both heroes are misfits, the tones of the two books are very different: Wain's veering between savage hostility to organized society and openly emotional yearning for a way out, Amis's a more lively, yet modest, mixture of the serious and the comic, and possessing what comes increasingly to look, almost thirty years later, like a pastoral innocence and charm in its depiction of Dixon and Christine's love relationship, and in its fascination—typical of the 1950s, and shown particularly in John Braine's *Room at the Top* (1957)—with the minutiae of provincial institutions and behavior. There is also, in Amis's novel, a far greater unity of structure: events take place over a short period and entirely within the academic and social world of Dixon's college. And where Wain's predominant influence is George Orwell, one may detect in *Lucky Jim* traces of Aldous Huxley and, even more, of the humorist P. G. Wodehouse. The hesitancies and shyness of Jim Dixon resemble those of Denis Stone in Huxley's *Crome Yellow* (1921), whose house-party framework itself may lie behind Dixon's arty weekend with the Welchs; certainly the arranged telephone call from Atkinson which frees Dixon from this distinctly resembles the device of the fake telegram by which Denis extricates himself from Crome. And in Anne's statement to Denis that "one enjoys the pleasant things, avoids the nasty ones. There's nothing more to be said" (*Crome Yellow*, Ch. 4) may lie the origin of "Nice things are nicer than nasty ones."

In view of Amis's reputation as a serious satirist—one which he has recently repudiated[21]—to compare him, in *Lucky Jim*, with such a delightfully frivolous writer as Wodehouse may seem strange. But he has himself mentioned reading Wodehouse's collection of letters, *Performing Flea* (1953), and his recognition in that work of a piece of advice he has followed: to give, from time to time, important speeches to minor characters.[22] The "pastoral innocence" which I have remarked on in *Lucky Jim* is an eminently Wodehousian quality, but there are closer parallels, in such a novel for instance as *Right Ho, Jeeves* (1934): not only the gushing talk of Madeline Bassett (which resembles Margaret Peel's avowals, like "How close we seem to be tonight, James. . . . All the barriers are down at last"), and the splendid speech given by Gussie Fink-Nottle at Market Snodsbury Grammar School as a result of "sixteen medium-sized gulps" of whiskey, and a jug of orange juice laced with gin (Ch. 16), but also the virtuosity and metaphoric elaboration habitual to Wodehouse's style, which seems to be in operation in Amis's description of Dixon's hung-over awakening in Chapter 6. Wodehouse also, like Amis, examines usage and modes of speech. Consider Bertie Wooster's anatomy of the exclamation "So!":

"So!" he said at length, and it came as a complete surprise to me that fellows ever really do say "So!" I had always thought it was just a thing you read in books. Like "Quotha!" I mean to say, or "Odds bodikins!" or even "Eh, ba goom!"

Still, there it was. Quaint or not quaint, bizarre or not bizarre, he had said "So!" and it was up to me to cope with the situation on those lines.

(*Right Ho, Jeeves*, Ch. 15)

Then place beside it Dixon's more concise but generically similar comment on Christine's use of the phrase "Uncle Julius":

... Dixon grinned to himself at "Uncle Julius." How marvellous it was that there should be somebody called that and somebody to call him that, and that he himself should be present to hear one calling the other that.

(*Lucky Jim*, Ch. 10)

It may well be, given its affinities both with Wain and with Wodehouse, that the immense popularity of *Lucky Jim* derives from its combination of the contemporary and the traditional, from its offering a vent for frustration together with a fundamental commonsense and good humor. We sympathize with Jim in his misfortunes, envy his eventual luck, and feel that, though he may not have the qualifications for his job with Gore-Urquhart, his virtues have deserved their reward.[23]

CHAPTER 3

Amis the Moralist

I That Uncertain Feeling *(1955)*

"LIFE, friends, is boring. We must not say so," complained the poet John Berryman. It is one of Amis's trademarks that he says so, and the *verismo* of his novels sometimes runs the risk of being boring as a result. Jim Dixon recommends himself to Gore-Urquhart (Ch. 21) as a "boredom-detector," and at the beginning of *That Uncertain Feeling* the boredom of life as an assistant librarian is transmitted by the versiclelike double repetition of the formula, spoken by the protagonist to a stupid patron in a "mitre-like hat," with which it opens: "The Bevan ticket . . . has expired, and will have to be renewed."

Amis's second novel follows a principle he has subsequently stuck to: "Always have another one going."[1] The writing of more than half of it overlapped with the writing of *Lucky Jim;* indeed, some elements almost suggest that Amis was writing *That Uncertain Feeling* with his other hand. Its hero, John Lewis, is twenty-six, about the same age as Jim Dixon; where Dixon is an assistant lecturer, Lewis is an assistant librarian; both are History graduates; Lewis's first encounter with his older temptress, Elizabeth Gruffydd-Williams, is preceded by a verbal trick that recalls Dixon and Professor Barclay: "Who she might be, and in addition who she was, remained obscure . . ." (Ch. 1); when Elizabeth declares to Lewis, in Chapter 9, "I desire you utterly," she sounds like Margaret Peel in "avowal" mood, and like Margaret Peel she has her neurotic side, the car accident she engineers in Chapter 16 being her version of a suicide attempt.

The fact, however, that this attempt is presented, rather than distantly recollected, in *That Uncertain Feeling*, and not only is presented but serves as a climax in its action, indicates the difference between Amis's second novel and his first. *That Uncertain Feeling*, though often funny, is a more painfully realistic novel; its "Aberdarcy" is derived from the Swansea Amis himself worked in; and Lewis's restricted circumstances as a young five-years-married man with two very young children are rendered with the verisimilitude of a writer similarly placed. Whereas Dixon's primary problem is his uncongenial job, from which he succeeds in escaping to the more exciting possibilities of London, Lewis's primary problem is his own divided nature, which he can master, it seems, only by moving from a large provincial town to a smaller, more remote one and by giving up the promotion to sublibrarian he had once wanted. If the ending of *Lucky Jim* feels like a victory for its protagonist, that of *That Uncertain Feeling*, though a sort of solution, is also a defeat.

The "uncertain feeling" of the title is described in Chapter 8 by John Lewis, who suffers from it. Having as its center a restless boredom, its other components are depression, uneasiness, and a "generalised lust" which finds its easiest outlet in watching attractive girls play tennis (Ch. 5) and looking clandestinely at bikinied pin-ups in tabloids like *Reveille*. Such activities seem harmless enough, and Amis's device of presenting events not only from Lewis's point of view but as his first-person narrative causes at least the male reader to sympathize with him: the depiction of his home life in Chapters 2 and 5 is certainly sordid enough, with its drying-rack and baby's rubber knickers and discarded toys, and for much of the novel the figure of his wife, Jean, the tired, thinning, and angular young mother who also suffers it, is barely noticed. Lewis's problem, however, is not sexual temptation; it is giving in to sexual temptation. He is "clear about" why he likes women's breasts (Ch. 5), but not about why he likes them "*so much,*" and his inordinate liking lays him open, as early as the first chapter, to "an old and hateful excitement" when he first encounters Elizabeth Gruffydd-Williams, rich, sophisticated, in her thirties, and married to a businessman with great influence on the affairs of the library committee. Despite his dislike of her milieu, and his naïve, rather priggish shock (Ch. 4) as he gradually realizes that her husband's influence may be brought to bear on behalf of his own candidacy for the vacant sublibrarianship, he cannot prevent himself drifting into an affair with Elizabeth. The force of his temptation is summarized by the rueful and funny exaggeration of Chapter 8: "One shouldn't catch sight of a woman . . . unless one intended to marry her."

The reference here to marriage and Lewis's description of his excitement as "hateful" give a further meaning to the "uncertain feeling" of the title. Much of the interest of the novel lies in its depiction of Welsh society and character, and it is plain from his essay "Where Tawe

Flows" (1954),[2] which describes a visit to the annual Eisteddfod, that Amis admired many aspects of Wales, of which he considered himself an adopted semicitizen. John Lewis is in part a role-playing, would-be Lothario, but he is also (and to this extent he is a surrogate for Amis himself[3]) a lower-middle-class Welshman with left-wing sympathies and residual Nonconformist instincts. He stands midway in the novel's spectrum between the rich, anglicized milieu of the Gruffydd-Williamses and their friends, "keen as mustard on culture," and the demotic Welshness variously represented by his own likable father, who works in the office of a colliery, by the worried and far less likable Ieuan Jenkins (his local, senior rival for the sublibrarianship), and by his neighbors the annoying, sentimental Mrs. Davies and her family. Where his lusts and boredom lead him into the first world, a mixture of instinctive loyalty and guilt keeps pulling him back toward the second.

It is typical of Amis that the choice is not easy, and it is far harder than in *Lucky Jim* for the protagonist to distinguish in practice the nice things from the nasty ones. John Lewis's dilemma is partly temperamental and partly cultural, in the broadest sense of the word, and it is further complicated by his wanting the job of sublibrarian, but not at the hands of Elizabeth or her husband, on whom it seems to depend. If Lewis, too unsophisticated to recognize Elizabeth's "gold tipped black fags" as Sobranie Black Russian cigarettes, moves in her world with far more truculent hostility than Dixon at his professor's arty weekend, he is no more easily able to relate to its extreme opposite, the pseudo-Welshness of Gareth Probert and his appalling verse play *The Martyr*, which provides Amis with ammunition for an attack on a different kind of cultural affectation. Despite his recent strenuous denial—"*Of course* Probert's not supposed to be Dylan Thomas"[4]— the verse of *The Martyr*, hilariously presented in Chapter 9, is not only clearly modeled on Thomas's early verse, with its word play[5] ("the son of dog"), but also steals from his later verse: "a grave truth" is taken straight out of "A Refusal to Mourn the Death, by Fire, of a Child in London" and the line "Crew junction down the sleepers of the breath" is surely modeled on "And blaspheme down the stations of the breath" from the same poem.[6] And its prose dialogue strongly recalls *Under Milk Wood*, "Llados" (sod all) being exactly the same type of inversion as Dylan Thomas's "Llareggub" (bugger all).[7]

The Martyr, in itself, is one of the two great "set pieces" of *That Uncertain Feeling*; nevertheless its author, Gareth Probert, in some ways unpleasantly reminiscent of Bertrand Welch, is shown behaving with dignity in the climactic Chapter 17, by which time Lewis has emerged from his affair with Elizabeth to face its consequences at home. Thus Amis is not merely indulging in digressive parody but suggesting how hard it is to see people fairly and in the round. The novel's other splendid set-piece, the "ideal interview" for the sublibrarianship devised by Lewis in Chapter 13 "to pass the time" while he waits in an anteroom for the real one, is related to the story even more tightly. Ostensibly, in its search for the dullest, most Welsh and least sexually tempted candidate ("Are you interested in women's breasts?" *My wife's a schoolteacher.*"), it is a virtuoso exercise in satirical, anti-Welsh hyperbole; yet a moment's reflection makes one realize that, in essentials, Lewis's colleague Ieuan Jenkins is the man it points to, and eventually it is he who gets the job. Lewis has felt sporadic but genuine guilt about Jenkins's claims, and at the end he is represented as only too glad not to have done Jenkins out of the raise in salary he desperately needs.

The real interview, long and horrible—and mercilessly observed— as it is, is rigged in Lewis's favor: Elizabeth wants him to get the job, as does her apparently complaisant husband for different reasons. Lewis has conscientiously (Ch. 13) not listened to Elizabeth's telephoned last-minute advice (he concentrates on reading a science-fiction story while she talks), trusting that if he is offered the job, it will be on his merits. Nevertheless—since by now his philandering has produced a perceptible coolness at home—he is glad enough to unwind after the interview with Elizabeth and her friends at a beach near Aberdarcy. Here, after a nude bathe, they finally make love: a curious, tender scene, not only in the lovemaking itself, but in the conversation that follows it, and in the symbolic purport of a sentence that precedes it: looking back across the bay at the lights of Aberdarcy, the usually nervous Lewis suddenly feels that "there was something to be happy about in being at the centre of so huge an area in the dark" (Ch. 15). It is the novel's least schematic, most lyrical moment, and for a while the relationship between Lewis and Elizabeth takes on genuine humanity and feeling—a considerable extension of the "cordiality and lack of tension" that mark their first kiss (Ch. 6).

Unfortunately, or fortunately, the feeling does not last. In Chapter 16, Lewis's moral objection to "fiddles," and hurt pride that the result of the interview was a foregone conclusion, combine with what he later admits to be fear of getting further involved with Elizabeth:[8] tenderness turns sour and argument escalates into a quarrel about principles and the decline of Lewis's marriage, which he regrets. Not without reason, one feels, does Elizabeth call him "mister chapel deacon," and whatever the rights and wrongs of the matter, Lewis is out of his depth in the complex situation created by his tendency to drift. Pulling out proves to be, for Lewis, the only course of action, and when as a result of the car "accident" Elizabeth's husband, suddenly protective of his errant wife, tells him not to "make any attempt to get in touch with her. Ever," he is only ensuring what Lewis has already decided.

The surprise made possible by Amis's use of first-person narrative springs its trap in Chapter 17. Looking at everything from his own point of view has caused Lewis effectively to ignore his wife's feelings about his affair, even while conveying compunction and, as it were, noticing her coolness out of the corner of his eye. His homecoming, after he has renounced both Elizabeth and the job, faces him with a jolt (and a slap). Jean, all along, has been a real person, suffering, her own simpler morality outraged by his unfaithfulness. He is faced, and deserves to be, by an operatic yet commonsensical tirade: to the insult of making love to Elizabeth he has added the injury of rejecting a job that is not simply his professional concern but the economic concern of his wife and children: if Ieuan Jenkins needs the money, so, surely, do they. The scene is one of the most dramatic in Amis's work, and when Lewis's own fear that he may have ruined what is most important to him—his marriage—drives him into the dark streets (which he fears, but fears less than his own realization that he must now decide something, since "there was nothing that could just happen") his disorientation and self-reproach take on a nightmarish vividness. When he accidentally "rescues" Ken Davies, the son of his detested downstairs neighbor, Mrs. Davies, the punch in the stomach he receives for his pains functions as a kind of expiation: as with the tea-leaves-swallowing incident in Chapter 8, "Life, that resourceful technician, had administered a typical rebuke." Rescuing Ken, lying hopelessly drunk in the street, is also the repayment of a debt (Ch. 10), since Ken and his father have both rallied to Lewis at awkward moments earlier in the novel; even more, this relatively selfless action serves to initiate Lewis's reintegration into the Welsh milieu in which, for all his previous strayings, he is really most at home.

This penultimate chapter, in which Lewis is brought face to face with the consequences of his "actions," is the novel's climax. It is perhaps a weakness of the novel that we are not shown how the reconciliation between Lewis and Jean is achieved: all we are told of is Lewis's determination, at last, "to keep trying not to be immoral" and his hope that "to keep trying might turn into a habit." Sufficient affection, of a modest domestic sort, has been indicated at various points, and behind Jean's anger is a hurt that can, perhaps, be assuaged by repentance. The move to the small colliery town of Fforestfawr,[9] and Lewis's new job in coal-sales revealed in the final, codalike chapter, have involved a slight reduction in Lewis's salary, but it appears that this is more than made up for by renewed harmony and a sense that, in returning to the town in which his father works, Lewis and his wife are among their own kind, almost able to be confused with the miners "coming off shift." And an earnest of Lewis's reformed behavior is furnished, if in rather undignified fashion, by his hasty retreat from the interest displayed in him by the Englishwoman Lisa Watkin at Mrs. Protheroe's cocktail party. This, Lewis feels, is where he came in; he is not staying for a repeat performance.

Such critics of Amis's work as David Lodge and Bernard Bergonzi have found it difficult to believe in Lewis's retirement to a town even smaller than the one in which he starts, into a pastoral world of working-class solidarity. There is, indeed, an irony to be noted in the contrast between the simple world Lewis has finally chosen and his sarcastic reflections earlier (Ch. 9) about "all those phony novels and stories about the wry rhetorical wisdom of poetical miners, all those boring myths about the wonder and the glory and the terror of life in the valley towns." Yet *That Uncertain Feeling* suggests throughout enough of Lewis's origins and affiliations in such an environment to make his return to it, after his disastrous venture into marital infidelity, credible enough, and it is its very credibility which is depressing, despite the jauntiness of the last chapter. The morality of "avoiding the occasion" is, one is forced to agree, better than no morality at all; but it is surely less challenging than to stay and fight, and is purchased at the expense of a more varied and potentially rewarding style of life. For all its frequent liveliness in the telling, John Lewis's is a sad story.

II   Take a Girl like You *(1960)*

There is much incidental humor in *That Uncertain Feeling*, both of situation—as when John Lewis, trapped in the Gruffydd-Williamses' house, first pretends to be a plumber and then escapes disguised as a woman in Welsh national dress—and of language—as in the accidental suggestiveness displayed when Lewis gets Vernon Gruf-fydd-Williams on the phone instead of Elizabeth:

"She did ask me to get hold of her specifically."
"Get hold of her what?" (Ch. 5)

Nevertheless, the novel's serious burden is not obscured by its amusement value, and Lewis's avoidance, at the end, of fresh temptation to adultery makes it easy to agree with Amis's description of himself in 1974: "I've always been a moralist."[10] It is the emergence of his wife as a real person, with hurt feelings, that finally makes Lewis try to follow his better, if duller, nature, and in *Take a Girl like You* it is as if Amis had decided to pursue the implication of this and acknowledge that in any situation of sexual morality two people, at least, are involved. Thus, throughout the novel, the problem of sexual morality, while giving rise to internal debate within the two main characters, Jenny Bunn and Patrick Standish, is externalized in a structure and narrative method that are dialectical. Each of the two characters broadly represents one moral viewpoint, and the action is presented (in the third person) through the eyes of each alternately, but with a bias toward Jenny: some fifteen chapters (including the first four and last three) reflect her attitudes, and some ten reflect Patrick's. The remaining two (Chs. 4 and 13) are in effect contests between them, statements of their two positions. This method of presentation allows the male reader to sympathize with Patrick, the female with Jenny; but it also forces both to acknowledge that mere partisanship is not adequate to a complex issue.

The issue in *Take a Girl like You* is that vexed one so dear to the 1950s: to make love or not to make love. Should a girl hang on to her virginity until marriage or should she succumb to male blandishments, parting with it earlier as an earnest of affection? In his poem "Annus Mirabilis"[11] Philip Larkin states categorically (and ruefully, since it was "far too late for me") that "Sexual intercourse began/In 1963." Amis's novel amounts to an investigation and summary of the uncertain decade which preceded this liberating, or immoral, simplification: a pre-Pill decade when to be in love brought with it, so often, a tug-of-war between physical instincts dangerous to satisfy and ingrained beliefs difficult to justify. Since Amis is of the same generation as Larkin, his view of the dilemma is by no means clear-cut, and though he began *Take a Girl like You* in Portugal in 1955, he set it aside in 1956 to write *I Like It Here,* knowing that the former novel "was going to take a long time to write"[12] and feeling that he "just wasn't mature enough to do" it at that time.[13]

It is clear from Amis's hesitations (he made about twelve drafts of the first chapter) that the subject was of great importance to him; it represented "a new departure,"[14] presumably in a technical sense, and on its appearance was felt to have struck a deeper vein of seriousness than its predecessors: its humor is almost entirely a matter of verbal formulae (e.g., Jenny's "lionhouse haddock" at the Thompsons' proliferating into "tea-towel beef," "rusty-knives steak pie," "cardboard chicken," and "dirty-dog mince"), and its ending is equivocal, even bleak. But the novel—the longest Amis has yet written—is also a large-scale rounding-out of his early interest in the role of sex in human relationships. The morality of extra- or premarital lovemaking per se is not pursued in later novels, let alone the importance of virginity, and now, twenty years later, the space and fuss devoted to it in *Take a Girl like You* may seem excessive. But, by that token, the novel is very much of its time, which is about 1958.

The novel is set in the South of England, in an unnamed "country town" near London whose features—canal, public school on a hill, a reference to Roman remains in the next town—suggest yet another appearance of Berkhamsted in Amis's work. If the atmosphere of the South in the late 1950s was characterized by rising affluence and declining rectitude, one of the period's literary elements was a view of the North of England as more old-fashioned, down-to-earth, and moral. Amis exploits this by making the male protagonist, Patrick Standish, an older, more educated, more sophisticated southerner, brought up in a south London suburb which sounds remarkably like Amis's Norbury (Ch. 11), and contrasting with him the ten-years-younger Jenny Bunn, who is working class and comes from "a large manufacturing city" in the North.[15] Her very name blends naïve charm and a shrewd, blunt practicality, and despite the decided limitations of her experience—she reads *Woman's Domain* and has no time for pieces of music called "Symphony No. 1 in C minor"—she is well able to "weigh people up" and, at least at first, to protect herself from the kind of passes her stunning good looks have the disadvantage of provoking.

The novel's title resembles the first line of a pop song, to which the phrase "and a boy like me" sounds the appropriate addition. However, despite the almost immediate mutual attraction felt by Jenny and Patrick, their ingredients take a long time to blend into a palatable dish, and even then it may seem to some only sweet-sour. No difficulty is made of their different backgrounds, tastes, and educational status—primary-school teacher, public-school master—nor is the ten-year age difference between them a problem in itself. Where the problem arises is in the handling of the physical attraction and in the assumptions that accompany it: Jenny instinctively thinks in terms of "saving herself," of marriage and children, and is in no rush to commit herself to much more than kisses; Patrick, a sports-car-driving bachelor of thirty with a number of liaisons behind him, sees Jenny primarily as a beautiful girl whom it would be a waste not to take to bed. Physically, one might say, they do not speak the same language, and the evening of their first date (Ch. 4) moves unsatisfactorily from a far too explicit pass by Patrick into a sequence of apologies, approaches, retreats, a lecture on the unimportance of virginity, and an inconclusive parting. When they meet again, ten days later (Ch. 8), Jenny's idyllic vision of a car-ride in the country with Patrick is all too soon shattered by the reality she sees in Julian Ormerod's enormous country house: Patrick kissing a girl he has only just met (Ch. 10).

The conflict between their sexual attitudes comes to a head in Chapter 13, when Patrick calls on Jenny in order to apologize, and an almost vulgar virulence ("All right, Mr. *Big Heart-Throb*") on her part is set against his self-justificatory demolition of her putative "Mr. Right": the kind of man who would combine attractiveness with sexual restraint before marriage. That kind, Patrick declares, "died in 1914 or thereabouts." Whether or not one agrees, Amis certainly presents no such type in *Take a Girl like You*, and when Jenny later goes out with Patrick's inept friend Graham McClintoch, Graham's long speech (Ch. 14) about the basic division of people into the attractive and the unattractive moves her to sympathize with him but at the same time underscores her preference for Patrick, with all his faults of insincerity and sexual greed.

The reconciliation which follows, and the loving but restrained relationship which ensues for some months, is made credible by aspects of Jenny and Patrick less doctrinaire than their commitment to virginity and seduction respectively. Though imagined to be "a veritable king of shaft" by the upper-class, free-wheeling Julian Ormerod (whose speech patterns, a mixture of sub-Wodehouse and ex-RAF slang, are one of the delights of the novel), Patrick's emotional preferences do not gibe with his sexual appetites: "the ones he liked were never the real stuff" (Ch. 11). And he still retains the residue of a youthful romanticism which is recalled in an evocative passage partly drawn, one feels, from Amis's own memories:

Was it really he who had spent a whole string of autumn evenings fifteen or sixteen years ago in the front room just off the London-Croydon road, playing his Debussy and Delius records by the open windows, in the hope that the girl who lived at the end of the street, and whom he had never dared speak to, would pass by, hear the music, look in and see him? Well, it was a good thing, and impressive too, that he could still feel a twinge of that uncompli- cated and ignorant melancholy. (Ch. 11)[16]

Jenny, though believing "she was the steady type who got married and had babies," also wonders at times whether the "starlet type" of girl doesn't have more fun (Ch. 4). She is too good-looking to escape the attentions of hopeful males of all kinds, but she not only notices their "looks" at her but also with unerring accuracy places them in ascend- ing order of attractiveness. Dick Thompson, her landlord, is a "stooge"; Graham is a "dud"; the amoral but likable and considerate Julian is a "near smasher"; and Patrick himself is a "smasher." Jenny combines inner purity (or, at least, knowing where to draw the line) with the kind of appearance which causes other women (the unhappily married Martha Thompson, the watchful and finally unpleasant headmistress Miss Sinclair, and the nice semitarts Susan and Wendy) to think she doesn't draw the line at all.

Patrick's pleasure trip to London with Julian (Chs. 17–20), which is described with a sociological zest for undue detail, is in part intended as a libertine experiment, in the light of which his tolerated semiceli- bacy with Jenny may be assessed. The strip shows leave him more or less cold, the first, followed as it is by the ghastly *double-entendres* of a northern comedian, proving "fully as exciting as looking up the word naked in the *Concise Oxford Dictionary.*" His encounter with the curt but beautiful "fashion model" Joan is more equivocal. Drink, and love for Jenny first render him incapable; but sexual attraction and bruised pride renew both interest and performance, and the pleasure and lack of "fuss" involved sharpen his impatience with "the old waiting game" (Ch. 20). So, too, one is left to infer, does Patrick's conversation with Lord Edgerstoune, which adds to his recurrent and very real fear of death an object lesson in the decline of sexual performance in old age.

It is in this frame of mind that Patrick issues his ultimatum to Jenny at the school cricket match: "I love you and I want to sleep with you.

I can't go on seeing you and not" (Ch. 22). From this point the momen-
tum of the novel increases, as Patrick's love, and his urge to get his
way, battle with Jenny's weakening principles and her fear of losing
him. Accepting his invitation "to be made an ex-virgin of," she nevertheless fails to turn up. As he waits for her to arrive, Patrick's antici-
patory excitement is succeeded by a passing regret at the fading of his
early research interests (Ch. 23), an intense nightmarish vision of his
own death accompanied by acute palpitations of the heart, relief at
"having been taken off Charon's quota for the day," and the arrival of
Sheila Torkington, who has got herself pregnant by the son of Patrick's
school enemy, Mr. Charlton. His unhesitating help to her in this situation is variously impressive—he arranges an abortion for her with
sympathy and efficient speed—but the lovemaking that precedes and
follows it, though understandable in view of Sheila's willingness and
Patrick's frustration, leaves him "feeling more ashamed and humili-
ated than he had ever felt in his life" (Ch. 24).

The emotional figurations of the last three chapters—set at Julian's
increasingly out-of-hand party and at Jenny's lodgings the following
morning—are extremely complex: a ballet of approach and retreat, of
tenderness and recrimination, of affection and power-tripping which
ultimately issues in an ending believable and human, if not uplifting.
The anticlimactic deflowering of Jenny when she is drunk cannot reasonably be described as a rape, but the flat, open syntax of its rendering
conveys very poignantly the emptiness of disappointment:

> ... she wanted him to stop, but her movements were all the wrong ones for
> that and he was kissing her too much for her to try to tell him. She thought
> he would stop anyway as soon as he realized how much off on his own he
> was. But he did not, and did not stop, so she put her arms round him and
> tried to be with him, only there was no way of doing it and nothing to feel.
> (Ch. 26)

One may sympathize with Julian's criticism of Patrick's lack of
"fairness,"[17] and with Patrick's postcoital self-disgust; he has indeed
gone too far, if only by spoiling the pleasure of an event likely by now
to occur without forcing. But Jenny herself has contributed to Patrick's
desperation by an earlier suggestion (Ch.25): instead of waiting for her
to come to him, Patrick should have taken all the responsibility on himself by collecting her and using "unfair" persuasion—precisely the
course to which her actions earlier in the novel had been most opposed.

At the end, driven back on her deepest feeling—her love for
Patrick—by the unprovoked hostility of Miss Sinclair, Jenny may well
feel it "rather a pity" that her "Bible-class ideas have . . . taken a
knocking": in gaining Patrick (all the evidence suggests they will now
marry[18]) she has certainly lost something of imprecise but real value to
her. Nevertheless, any feeling that Patrick has "won" is counterbal-
anced by the more general exasperation he expresses at the whole mess
of courtship in the unsettled moral atmosphere of the 1950s: "You can't
win at this bloody game, can you?" (Ch. 25). Amis may indeed have
intended the ending of *Take a Girl like You* to be "a kind of lament
. . . for the passing of that great set of certainties" which included (contradictorily enough) "powerful but very vague ideas of right and
wrong,"[19] and the cavalcade it offers of 1950s sexual mores and socio-
cultural patterns is almost oppressively dense and detailed. But given
the fact that, despite their hindering preconceptions as to how the
"game" of love should be acted out, Patrick and Jenny are left at the
conclusion with each other, perhaps the aptest moral the novel offers
is the casual remark made by the easygoing Wendy when she is questioned by Jenny at Julian's party:

"Do you think it's right to give up your principles for somebody you're in
love with?"
    "I don't know anything about principles. They just make life harder, don't
they?" (Ch. 26)

CHAPTER 4

The Amis Hero and "Abroad"

A N important characteristic of some of the writers who emerged in the 1950s is their suspicion of "abroad," of foreign countries and of foreigners. Philip Larkin was once asked, in a literary questionnaire, whether he read foreign poetry. His answer was short and scathing: "*Foreign* poetry? No."[1] Kingsley Amis, commenting on the shortcomings of his own generation of poets, spoke of their "meagreness and triviality of subject matter" and asserted that, while "nobody wants any more poems on the grander themes for a few years," at the same time "nobody wants any more poems about philosophers or paintings or novelists or art galleries or mythology or foreign cities or other poems. At least I hope nobody wants them."[2] It is in this spirit—a reversal of the Europeanness of writers like E. M. Forster—that one should take Garnet Bowen's objection, at the beginning of *I Like It Here,* to the idea of visiting Italy: "All those rotten old churches and museums and art galleries."

In part this "Little Englandism," as its detractors have called it, is a species of lower-middle-class defensiveness: the preference for the home-grown of those who must rely on it, the transposed envy of the package tourist for the elegant fluency displayed by modern heirs of the "Grand Tour." It is also a version of the dislike of affectation, since, it might be claimed, the extreme form of affectation is speaking a language other than English. Obviously such attitudes, capable of exaggeration if not already exaggerated, offer much ammunition to the comic or seriocomic novelist. But they have a more positive side: to prefer "abroad" may be no more than cultural snobbery, to "like it here" no less than common sense. Three of Amis's novels, published between 1958 and 1968, are set partly or wholly outside England, and demonstrate with greater or lesser degrees of emphasis the confrontations of protagonists, more or less sympathetic, with alien ways of thought and behavior. Since, as well as being set "abroad," the three novels are fairly short and comparatively lightweight, it is convenient to deal with them in a single chapter.

I   I Like It Here *(1958)*

In 1955 Amis stayed for some time in Portugal, having been obliged to go abroad by the stipulations of the Somerset Maugham prize, which he had won for *Lucky Jim*. While there he began to write *Take a Girl like You*, but set this aside for reasons indicated in Chapter 3. Instead, Amis's third novel to be published, written in 1956, was a loose fictionalization of the visit to Portugal itself, which gave him the opportunity to exorcise, to laugh at, and also, at the end, to defend his xenophobia: the initials of his hero, Garnet Bowen, are near his own in the alphabet, but they are also, appropriately, those of Great Britain, as displayed on the number-plate of the car Bowen takes with him.

At least an equally important element in the novel is its exploration of the contrast between Amis's generation of writers and the "great novelists" born two or three decades earlier—the generation which included Amis's unwitting benefactor Somerset Maugham, to whom a number of references, mocking yet tactful, are made in the course of it. Though the novel's manner is notably light and casual, and its details often seem a hasty transcription of notes jotted down on the spot, Amis's comment on it—it "has very little to say about anything"[3]—is too modest. The truce it proclaims with different places, different styles, the reluctant but real broadening of horizons which it arrives at, the presentation—unique in Amis's novels—of a happy married relationship which it offers "without" (in the words Amis applies to Fielding in Ch. 15) "evangelical huffing and blowing," all these make it one of Amis's most satisfying novels, and certainly his most good-humored. The exasperation with which it seethes is so exaggerated that the reader is clearly expected, while sympathizing, not to take it seriously: "Perhaps it was all to do with architecture. Oh, how he loathed architecture. He would have liked to see it all done away with" (Ch. 3).

I Like It Here is also Amis's most literary novel. Its hero, Garnet Bowen, with his engaging paranoia about architecture, going abroad, and airplanes, is a writer who uneasily combines journalism, lecturing, and costive attempts to complete his play *Teach Him a Lesson* with an unwillingness to be caught saying anything of a cultural sort in other than an ironical way. Even if he does wish it "further and further behind him," the punning title of his one book, *No Dogmas Allowed*, typifies him as a 1950s writer: that is, someone who has espoused the vocation of writing but who repudiates any of the "phoney," convo-

luted sensitivity and sense of the writer's high calling which marks the
work of such a one as Wulfstan Strether, the recluse expatriate novelist
whose identity Bowen's trip to Portugal is among other things concerned with establishing. Double-edged as ever, Amis's irony "places"
Strether's artiness by the titles he invents for his novels: *Rapid Falcons,
Mad as the Mist and Snow*, the Shakespearean pretensions of *This
Rough Magic*, and *One Word More*, the prolix manuscript of which
Bowen carries with him to Portugal. As his ship pauses at Cherbourg,
Bowen's flat, grudging, irritated perception of France and what he
takes it to stand for expresses with splendid economy his twin objec-
tions to abroad and to literary pretentiousness:

He looked out of the window at what could be seen of France: a bit of wall,
a drum or tub of something, a van. But this appearance of inertia did not
deceive him. He knew that they were all there really, all on duty demonstrating to one another their capacity for logic, their wit and grace, their responsible and informed interest in politics, their high regard for Poe and Charles
Morgan. God, yes. . . . (Ch. 4)

Similar literary preconceptions at first dog Bowen's arrival in Portugal: "It would be unendurable if [the peasants] all turned out to be
full of instinctive wisdom and natural good manners and unself-con-
scious grace and a deep, inarticulate understanding of death" (Ch. 5).
In fact, he finds he enjoys the place, despite insects, stomach upsets,
and the cramped and unduly expensive quarters near Estoril in which
they are at first housed by the Oateses: the drink is cheap, the natives
are friendly, and the days "full of splendidly straightforward sunshine"
(Ch. 7). Much of the novel's first half is concerned with local impressions and local characters—Harry Bannion, the Catholic Ulsterman
retired from a bank in India, is an especially bravura creation, with his
fantastic floridities of speech (which recall the "Museyroom" section of
Joyce's *Finnegans Wake*[4]) and his elaborate recitation of "The Charge
of the Light Brigade": surely a Dickensian, larger-than-life creation
drawn from life. Similarly remote from any concern with plot is the
case for Dr. Salazar (efficiency), put by the lower-middle-class Oates,
and the case against him (censorship, repression) put by the upper-
class, sophisticated Gomes, whom Bowen meets in a bar.

The gloomy picture Gomes presents is slyly used by Amis to offset
the left-wing sympathies espoused by Bowen: "A penumbra of trivial

insularity had been pretty effectively cast over British domestic squab-
bles about housing policy or the next round of wage claims. . . . Gomes
seemed to have provided yet another excuse for people like Bowen to
be politically apathetic at home" (Ch. 8). Lest this reflection seem critical of Bowen, it should be related to what Amis said in 1957 in *Socialism and the Intellectuals:* "politics [in Britain] have become, and seem
all too likely to remain, unromantic."[5] It would seem that Bowen's
realization leads naturally to that of Amis, who elsewhere links himself
with his protagonist by giving him a Swansea provenance, three children (*I Like It Here* is dedicated to Amis's three children), a liking for
the novels of Elizabeth Taylor, and driving experiences in Germany in
1945.

Insofar as anything holds the novel together, it is Bowen's developing
relationship with the novelist John Wulfstan Strether, as his full name
is finally discovered to be; though until Bowen is certain he is not an
imposter he is referred to as "Buckmaster." He is the generic expatriate
writer of an earlier generation, belonging to a patrician world quite
unfamiliar to Bowen, and therefore suspect. He is an identikit figure:
the shape of his name suggests John Cowper Powys, his situation that
of Norman Douglas in Italy, Robert Graves in Majorca, Maugham at
Cap Ferrat—Strether's house is one in which "any whisky-sodden tea-
planter or homicidal adulteress would have felt at home" (Ch. 7). But
though "his dialogue recalled Charles Morgan rather than anything
Downing College would approve,"[6] his closest analogue is Henry
James: "Strether" is the protagonist of *The Ambassadors*, and the style
of *One Word More*—a set-piece of Amisian pastiche (Ch. 9)—resembles the opening pages of that novel clearly enough.

Though Bowen, reasonably, never manages to approve of his last
novel, or of the "English Men of Letters Series eloquence" (Ch. 15) of
his "conversation," Strether's amiability and Old-World courtesy soon
win him over, and though his mission makes him try to remain sceptical he seems rarely in doubt as to his host's genuineness, both in being
who he claims to be, and in being, for all the long-windedness of his
style, convinced of the importance of his calling and of the value of his
contribution to literature. As Chapter 9 makes painfully clear,
Strether's novels exist, whereas Bowen's play can barely inch its way,
self-consciously, on to the page.

Bowen's involvement with Strether culminates in their visit to Fielding's tomb in Chapter 15. It is a visit, Bowen suddenly realizes, that he
is eager to make, though his embarrassment at such "non-ironical"

respect for a literary master grumbles in a characteristic face-saving
thought: "He could keep quiet about it when he got home." Strether
also respects Fielding, as a fellow-practitioner, but declares the superiority of his own tragic fiction to "the utterances of comedy, whatever
their purity or power." It is this statement, vainer than any impostor
would dare make, which sets the official seal, as it were, on Buckmaster's identity as Strether, in terms of the story; but it is clear that Amis's
preference, like Bowen's, is for Fielding—"the only non-contemporary
novelist who could be read with unaffected and whole-hearted interest." It is also clear that Amis's admiration for the comic master is
related to admiration for his "moral seriousness" and mixed with envy
for the clarity of his "simplified world": " . . . how enviable to live in
the world of his novels, where duty was plain, evil arose out of malevolence and a starving wayfarer could be invited indoors without hes-
itation and without fear."

However, Bowen's alignment with the sensible values of Fielding
does not preclude a personal liking for Strether, and it is his admiration
for a world "where duty was plain," the reader may feel, that enables
him to overcome his fear of driving and fetch help for Strether, despite
all the frustrations of the Portuguese language, when he has been
knocked down by his temperamental chauffeur. Thus, if the close of
the novel shows Bowen glad to be back in the gray England of "Sorry-
sir," glad to be reunited with his wife (who, unlike the beautiful
Emilia, "could never conceivably be a blackmailer's girl"), and unsure
how far an experience of abroad is an experience of life at firsthand,
there is little doubt that he has learned some valuable lessons in seriousness and tolerance: it is as if, in this novel, some belated justice were
being done to the values represented by Professor Welch's "arty"
weekend. As Bowen's wife lightly but truly remarks at the end: "I
think your holiday's done you a lot of good."

II   One Fat Englishman *(1963)*

I Like It Here is, in all senses, a holiday novel. *One Fat Englishman*,
not its immediate successor but the successor of *Take a Girl like You*,
is a much more bitter book, lightweight only in length, and certainly
not in the size and nature of its protagonist, the sixteen-stone publisher
Roger H. St. John W. Micheldene, greedy in all his appetites and pre-
cariously poised on the sharp edge of his own outrage. It is an interesting coincidence that Amis's fifth novel, essentially a study of Roger

Micheldene's unhappy temperament, appeared at about the same time as a newspaper piece by a British black humorist not unlike Amis, Michael Frayn. Some lines in it fortuitously hit off Micheldene's dominant "humour":

How rich the world was in resentment! For a moment he had a brilliantly clear vision of the universe as a network of interlocking resentments. Everyone resented everyone. Even the beam, he saw with strange clarity, must resent his head, and his head the beam.
[. . . .]
Only resent, he thought. If we didn't resent, some of us wouldn't know we were alive.[7]

In 1973 Amis described Patrick Standish as "the most unpleasant person I've written about."[8] But in 1974 he described Roger Micheldene as "undoubtedly the most unpleasant of my leading characters."[9] Revealingly, he added: "I like Roger," who is "your" [i.e., my] "idea of yourself if you pushed a bit of it to an extreme." Roger Micheldene is a more unpleasant character than Patrick Standish, having his sexual greed,[10] his emotional calculatingness, and his hostility in greatly increased measure. Patrick, relieving his remorse, shoots Dick Thompson; Roger, escaping his self-disgust, shoves Father Colgate's face into his fish tank (Ch. 13); but Roger's attitude to the world at large is resentful, and much of the world, recognizing this, resents him back. One might say that Roger is what Patrick would have festered into if he had not succeeded in capturing Jenny.

But this is not entirely fair. As Amis has stated, "being a bastard and realizing it is a kind of cross which he bears," and though Amis's third-person viewpoint sometimes holds Roger up, aloofly, for the reader's condemnation, it more frequently sees the world through his eyes and elicits the reader's sympathy, if not his approval. If Roger often behaves badly—and his butting a West Indian author in the stomach (Ch. 7) is recalled deliberately to show how bad, and how childish, his behavior can be—those he meets do not always behave well to him. Irving Macher, the clever Jewish student and author of *Blinkie Heaven*, who tests Roger's reactions by various joky experiments, is an odd-ball and a "smart-ass"; and if he tolerates "indulgently" Roger's excesses when provoked, the provocation itself is an impertinence to an older man. Roger's individual "awfulness" persuades the reader to accept the truth of Macher's declaration in Chapter 16: "It isn't your nationality we don't like, it's you"; but the emphasis this gains by being placed right at the end of the chapter does not cancel the different emphasis of the novel's title. Roger's personal problem is his tenuous relationship with Helene Bang, "a slim girl with an endearingly disproportionate bosom" (Ch. 1); but he also represents, in however exaggerated a form, the English end of the often suspicious relationship between two countries "divided by a common language." Somewhere behind Roger's sullenly blazing encounters with New York and the sarcastically named Budweiser College lie Amis's own experiences as a Visiting Fellow (like his philologist Ernst Bang) at Princeton in 1958–59;[11] he has remarked that the novel "caused no end of trouble in Princeton. They were all busy trying to identify themselves."[12] The tenor of Roger's caustic, post-Waughian observations of his "abroad," America, may be undercut by the nasty nature of their sixteen-stone vehicle, but the observations are made nonetheless, and with savage gusto. Amis the moralist has his cake, but Amis the satirist eats it.

Amis does not fictionalize his American visit in quite the direct, quasi-reportorial way he employs for Portugal in *I Like It Here*, though Roger's visits, in Chapter 15, to various New York jazz joints are less a necessity of plot than they are a perfunctory gesture of authorial piety. Rather he allows it to furnish the background, a constantly irritating one, for his upper-class protagonist Roger Micheldene—a distinctly "invented" surrogate, as the contrast with Pargeter in Chapter 4 seems designed to show—and for the quest he is hopelessly involved in. Micheldene is not a lecturer staying in America for some time, but a publisher, visiting it briefly in the late October of 1962, with various incidental professional errands but a more urgent personal one: to meet and possibly to entice away from her husband, and even perhaps to marry, a woman of twenty-nine he has loved since 1957, seen briefly on a few occasions, and slept with once in London, in April 1961. He has only sixteen days to make a strong enough impression, and if his pursuit of Helene Bang degenerates as a result into a greedy grasping at the few opportunities for sex with her, the prehistory of Roger's feelings, sketched in carefully in the first few chapters, adds to it a moving element of desperation. There is, certainly, something more than lust in his frustrated maneuverings to obtain a full frontal view of her in her bikini beside the Derlangers' pool.

The question, however, is how much greater that something is, and whether it can prevail over other elements in Roger's nature. "Of the seven deadly sins, Roger considered himself qualified in gluttony, sloth and lust, but distinguished in anger" (Ch. 1). The course of his meetings with Helene, at the Derlangers', at Budweiser, and finally in New York, makes it clear to Helene and to the reader that his anger is too strong. His pettish reaction to "The Game" (Ch. 4), in which he insists that the charade on the adverb "Britishly" is designed to mock him, provokes her silent "contempt," and no qualifying comment invites the reader to disagree. His selfish reaction to their lost opportunity for lovemaking at Hallowe'en (Ch. 5) provokes her to complain, as much for his sake as her own, about his anger. And when finally (Ch. 11) they do manage to make love, in a scene whose elements of tenderness are not diminished by Roger's reciting Virgil, Greek verbs, and A. E. Housman to himself in order to delay climax and prolong his pleasure, their brief moment of real communication is ruined not by the arrival of Roger's lecture, stolen by Macher and now returned by him, but by Roger's resultant anger: minutes left for love are sacrificed in a futile attempt at revenge.

Other factors militate, for the reader, against Roger's deserving to succeed with Helene: his two bouts of sex with Mollie Atkins, his pass—parried by a bite—at Irving Macher's girl Suzanne (Ch. 12), both of which courses are prompted by lust per se and setbacks with Helene. And in the event it proves, anyway, that for all her occasional straying, as with Macher in New York (Ch. 16), she is happy with her tolerant husband, the one man, she feels, who sees her and likes her for herself. At most, her feeling for Roger has been one of erratic sympathy and guilt. One cannot blame her; yet Roger's tears in his cabin (Ch. 17) are genuine: insofar as he can love anyone, he has loved Helene, and in his lovemaking "he came as close as he had ever done to being unaware of who he was" (Ch. 11).

Who Roger is is someone not very pleasant. He takes offense too easily, chokes off barmen and taxi-drivers, is far from displaying "old world courtesy" when he finally discards Mollie Atkins (Ch. 13), and is meaner than is called for to that dreaded "monologuist and domestic acrobat" (Ch. 10), Arthur Bang, who is a direct descendant of the boy "of unjustifiable appearance" noticed by Garnet Bowen on his voyage to Lisbon. To have one's lecture stolen is certainly a poor joke, but to cancel one's appearance as a result is an overreaction, and when the bland, blandly named Father Colgate tells Roger that "a man doesn't act like a child unless his soul is hurting him" (Ch. 9), one is obliged to agree. But Father Colgate's meliorist simplicities are rather repellent, and Roger's reply to them in Chapter 8 has a perverse cogency: "We're bound to God by ties of fear and anger and resentment as well as love." It is an appropriately Greene-esque attitude from a character who is a bad Catholic and has been educated at Graham Greene's school, Berkhamsted.

But stressing this element is perhaps to spiritualize the novel too much. Roger Micheldene is also, in his angry-middle-aged-man way, very funny, in the outrageous manner of Evelyn Waugh when he refers to California, in *The Loved One* (1948), as "the barbarous regions of the world" and its suburban noises as "the ever present pulse of music from the neighbouring native huts." There is an engaging directness in Roger's peppery reaction to things American which appeals to the primitive hostility in any reader: Roger's linguistic refusal to admit an expression like "ticker-tape" (Ch. 4), or the word for what Joe Derlanger, in Chapter 1, is wearing on his feet—"what Roger had heard called sneakers"; his blind prejudice to American-ness in itself, encountered on his train journey into Pennsylvania: "The train, though fast and not barbarously uncomfortable, had been full of Americans." Amis derives a more subtle, if no less nasty, humor from setting the reality of Roger's first encounter with the Budweiser students against his stereotyped expectations, so that the students seem merely the exception that proves the rule:

> None of them was chewing gum or smoking a ten-cent cigar or wearing a raccoon coat or drinking Coca-Cola or eating a hamburger or sniffing cocaine or watching television or mugging anyone or, perforce, driving a Cadillac. Quite a little minority culture group. (Ch. 7)

Given the way America treats him, it seems only fair that, by way of reward for his otherwise pointless pursuit of Helene to Strode Atkins's New York flat, he should (idly reading a note from L. S. Caton in the process) discover and repatriate a Swinburne notebook, appropriately concerned with flagellation. Given the way he treats America, it is fair also that, for the journey back, he should have an American for unwelcome companion, and that, by a twist of irony, it should be Strode Atkins. The ending, suggesting a living death like that of Tony Last reading Dickens to Mr. Todd in Waugh's *A Handful of Dust*, is a sour joke apt to the tone of the whole novel: an Englishman who lets down the image of his country is closeted with an American who gets Anglophilia a bad name.

III   I Want It Now (1968)

The seed of Ronnie Appleyard, the trendily named thirty-six-year-old columnist of the *Sunday Sun*, compère of the discussion program "Insight," and reluctant hero of *I Want It Now*, can be found in a short description in *I Like It Here*, which compares two photographs, early and late, of Garnet Bowen: "The 1956 Bowen was twice as wide and had something of the air of a television panellist. His question about *Aaron's Rod* would have concerned how much money whoever wrote it had made out of it" (Ch. 3). And the disdainful lady with "blackbird-plumage hair" whom Bowen expects to meet at Buckmaster's house is perhaps the first stirring of Ronnie's dragonish adversary with "blackbird hair," Lady Baldock, whose carapace of riches is described, on her first appearance, with Wodehousian panache: "There was a kilogram or so of jewellery and a heavy dry white silk dress, the bodice of which had evidently been sprayed with glue and fiercely bombarded with diamonds." The girl for whose possession they duel, Simona Quick, is beautiful in a way which would have attracted Roger Micheldene, "a face-fetichist of many years' standing": Ronnie's first view of her face at the Reichenbergers' party prompts him to think "it might be the most attractive face he had ever seen." The strength of Ronnie's reaction, indirectly conveyed, is in inverse proportion to the understated plainness of Amis's language.

If these basic ingredients of *I Want It Now* were lying about for some years, what brought them together, or at any rate gave them an operational context, was Amis's greater familiarity, since leaving academic life in 1963 and coming to London, with the cosmopolitan world of the "media," and two specific trips: one to the southern states of America, to teach at Vanderbilt University in Nashville some time in 1967–68; the other a little earlier, to gather material for a new "James Bond" novel he had been invited to write: *Colonel Sun*, published the same year as *I Want It Now*. The latter trip involved him in taking "a fifty-foot converted fishing boat from Piraeus to the islands of Naxos and of Ios";[13] it is not difficult to recognize in these islands of the Cyclades the origin of "Malakos, Poustos," the locale for section two of Ronnie's odyssey. The former trip furnished him with the southern mansions, and the southern accents, of section three, though "Fort Charles" itself (geographically) seems to be based on Atlanta, Georgia, rather than on Nashville, Tennessee.

Continuing the new pattern inaugurated in *The Anti-Death League* (1966), *I Want It Now* is not divided old-fashionedly into a fairly large number of chapters, often more than one of them to a single situation or setting, but into a smaller number of large sections which enable the overall structure of the novel to be seen more clearly. There are four, the first and last of them set in London, the glamorous, unpleasant world of commercial television in which Ronnie earns his salary, the central ones set in the "abroad," both literal and metaphorical, of the international superrich—a "real small circle," as George Parrot calls it, whose money derives from the work, present or past, of others. What brings Ronnie into that world is his pursuit, first motivated by the scent of money, then by a kind of sexual missionary zeal, then by love, of Simona Quick, the strange twenty-six-year-old rich girl whose apparent nymphomania is in fact an overcompensation for hatred of sex.

Part of Simona's problem is indicated by the variant forms of her name: boyish in figure, she acts aggressively and calls herself "Simon," but to her dominating mother, the thrice-married Lady Baldock, she is "Mona," submissive, silent, and conned. This "mixed-up" element in her—she even has two ways of speaking, one normal-to-lively, the other a dispirited, laconic grunt—counterbalances the "swinging 'sixties" aspect of her surface promiscuity, with its slogan "I want it now."[14] The reader gradually realizes that what is on one level the patient induction of a frigid girl into the new world of the orgasm is on another a fairy tale of romance: the rescue of a princess held in the evil spell of her witch-mother by the determination and courage of a "shit" who gradually discovers he is a better person than he thought. Amis reveals this element in the story quite openly in the final section by making a reference to the legend of the Sleeping Beauty; even in the first, though with no apparent truth at the time, Ronnie Appleyard is described as "TV's Young Lochinvar."

A little before the period in which *I Want It Now* was written, Amis had made his political switch from an instinctive but uncertain socialism to a "grudging toleration of the Conservative Party."[15] Amis's waverings can be felt in the political cast of his heroes from the late 1950s onward: Patrick Standish supports the Labour party, Roger Micheldene is a Tory bigot, but both enjoy a measure of sympathy from their creator. Ronnie Appleyard is Amis's first "trendy Lefty," espousing fashionable Socialist causes (such as anti-*apartheid*) without caring more than factitiously because "Left politics were . . . the route of advancement" and Ronnie's goal, at the beginning, is "fame and money, with a giant's helping of sex thrown in." His snide maneuverings as a TV "personality," both on his own program and with his senior and even snider colleague Bill Hamer, are as sharply observed as they are meanly performed, and his initial involvement with Simona, once he has discovered she is an heiress, is a calculated business: in his mind the words "Eaton Square" and "penthouse" "rang . . . like a great cash register." On all counts, he seems hardly a Lucky Jim.

And yet, as Ronnie's excursions into the yacht-and-villa world of the superrich make clear, *I Want It Now* bears a strong general resemblance to Amis's first novel. If Ronnie at first seems what Lord Baldock thinks him—a fortune-hunter "on the chisel"—the rich whom he encounters on Malakos and Poustos are so much worse that by comparison he seems innocent, vulnerable, and sensitive. The meanness of the rich—their "Stilton-paring"—over liquor and food is rendered in incredulous, contemptuous detail, as is the tastelessness of their décor and their lack of tolerance for the opinions of others. Lady Baldock is in this particular respect a super-Bertrand, and Ronnie finds himself no longer welcome on her yacht as a result of differing with her, very politely, over Simona, who for all her numerical experience with men resembles Christine in being unduly under the influence of someone older and ruthless. By the end of section two, Ronnie has realized, to his surprise, that he *loves* Simona, and his sexual therapy—described with reticence and seriousness[16]—has brought her to "absolutely the first time it's ever not been horrible."

The private battle, won by patience, is succeeded in section three by the public one—getting Simona away from her mother, who tolerates her "affairs" but will only admit as her husband someone equally rich. Ronnie has ousted her first suitor, George Parrot, in section one; Parrot's "Dixie" accent provides Amis with one of his best linguistic jokes, a translation of his sounds into meaningful words which yet make no sense: "Ah, Apollo jars. Arcane standard, Hannah More. Armageddon pier staff." ("I apologise. I can't stand it any more. I'm a-getting pissed off.") Parrot proves unexpectedly magnanimous in section three in helping Simona to run away with Ronnie, peremptorily dismissed by Lady Baldock from her southern mansion, to which he has come in search of Simona after a three-month separation. Three incidents at Fort Charles reveal the new seriousness of Ronnie's character, all of them connected with Student Mansfield ("There was nothing under the sun that an American could not be called."), Simona's new, mother-approved, rich racist suitor. One is his genuine disgust at George Parrot's story about Manfield's nefarious, unofficerlike conduct in Germany in 1955; another is his shock at hearing from Simona that she has actually slept with Mansfield (a shock deliberately conveyed by cliché—the glass he is holding slides out of his nerveless hand); the last is his attack of "pure, authentic, violent sentiment of a liberal or progressive tendency" when he confronts Mansfield's anti-Negro statements with a loud "Balls." This gives Lady Baldock the excuse to "have things the way I want them" in her own house, and even the lovers' subsequent escape to "Old Boulder National Park"—described with almost Nabokovian interest in domestic Americana—is interrupted by the police. In his "away" match with the rich, Ronnie seems to have met defeat.

A variety of factors, too many to detail, allow him a final victory on "home" ground. By a clever piece of authorial structuring, the last section, set like the first in London, shows Ronnie's mean interviewing techniques harnessed to the good purpose of showing up the arrogant authoritarianism of Lady Baldock on the "Bill Hamer programme." Aided by Hamer, Ronnie is able to contrive it so that he both denounces Lady Baldock himself and goads her to speak so openly in reply that she is excluded from further participation in the program. Moral triumph, however, is only turned into practical victory by the deus-ex-machina intervention of Lord Baldock, who has finally realized that Ronnie loves Simona, not her money. (No one who spoke against Lady Baldock in public would ever get Simona's money, held in trust, anyway.) Living up, finally, to his sobriquet of "Chummy," and indulging vicariously his own defiance of his wife, he brings the lovers together in the best tradition of romantic novels of elopement.

On the personal level, the ending of *I Want It Now* is credible: Simona and Ronnie, each imperfect, have improved each other and seem likely to continue this process. The ending is also realistic in that the motives which involve Hamer and Lord Baldock in aiding, and the "ritz" Greek Vassilikós in approving, the defeat of Lady Baldock, have a strong admixture of (well-merited) spite toward her. The ending also illustrates Amis's political eclecticism: he has allowed Ronnie his liberal gesture of defiance to the merely rich, but he balances this "pinko" element (George Parrot's word) by ensuring that Simona be brought to

Ronnie by a crusty English peer—poor but honest—who (like Evelyn Waugh) is a member of the very conservative White's Club. Nevertheless, for all these touches that locate the novel in a world of believable human types, and in the gray Britain of *"Export Gap Widens . . . Textile Strike Spreads," I Want It Now*—and no less enjoyably for that—is a work of romantic, fairy-tale optimism, in which love conquers all, even the element of drifting passivity in its heroine. At the end, she is only a month or so off a fashionable Knightsbridge wedding when "TV's Young Lochinvar" spirits her away.

CHAPTER 5

Amis's God

I   The Anti-Death League (1966)

TWO of the "nonsensical" phrases spoken by George Parrot in *I Want It Now* might almost have been designed by Amis to refer back to its immediate predecessor, *The Anti-Death League.* "Apollo jars" and "Armageddon pier staff" have a sinister aptness to that novel's revelations of germ warfare, to be waged by the picked officers of "Operation Apollo" as a countermeasure to a projected Chinese invasion of the Indian subcontinent. *I Want It Now* appeared in the same year, 1968, as Amis published his sequel to Ian Fleming's James Bond novels, *Colonel Sun*, so entitled after its Chinese villain. In his essay "A New James Bond," also published in 1968, Amis explained his authorship of *Colonel Sun* as the outcome of a long-standing attraction toward "genre" fiction—ghost, horror, spy, and crime stories: "I had always vaguely wanted, and for some time had been a little more purposefully intending, to write a thriller. When the Bond thing came up, it seemed like a gift from the gods."[1] The existence of *Colonel Sun* notwithstanding, one may reasonably claim that the large spy-thriller element in *The Anti-Death League* makes it, in fact, the first example in Amis's work of genre fiction.

The Anti-Death League is, however, more than this. Amis has described it as "my favourite of my own books. Partly because of being more ambitious than anything before."[2] The military spy-thriller provides the necessary framework of story within which Amis attempts to fuse and intensify motifs present in two previous novels: the God—a resented God—who is mentioned for the first time in *One Fat Englishman*, and the view of providence indicated in passing, in *Take a Girl like You,* by Patrick Standish's notion "Bastards HQ." The "malicious malevolent"[3] God fully unveiled by *The Anti-Death League* is broadly in line with Amis's essay of 1962, "On Christ's Nature," in which he approves the hostility evinced toward the "very

63

wicked . . . traditional God of Christianity" by William Empson in
Milton's God (1961). Another essay by Amis, also published in 1962,
expresses this Hardyesque attitude by means of an actual conversa-
tional exchange between himself and the visiting Russian poet Yevgeny
Yevtushenko:

> "You atheist?" he asked me in English.
> "Well yes, but it's more that I hate him."[4]

The baldness of this statement obliges the reader of *The Anti-Death
League* to see in the views of James Churchill, the twenty-four-year-
old subaltern trained for "Operation Apollo," much that speaks for his
older author, but the use of multiple viewpoints—an extension of the
technique of *Take a Girl like You*—prevents the final effect of the
novel from being simplistic.

The Anti-Death League, being concerned with what might be
called man's existential state, is more obviously serious than Amis's pre-
ceding five novels, and its seriousness is conveyed not only by an
absence from it of funny incidents but by a spare simplicity, indeed a
somberness, of style which eschews linguistic mannerisms and literary
references. In this it differs from the earlier novels, but resembles
Amis's three short stories of army life, "My Enemy's Enemy," "Court
of Inquiry," and "I Spy Strangers," which were written in the 1950s
but first collected in *My Enemy's Enemy* in 1962. The sobriety of the
novel can thus be related not only to its bleak vision of "divine providence," but also to Amis's desire for verisimilitude in his military setting. It is noticeable that none of the officers (except Colonel White,
too minor a character, who reads French existentialists) is the sort of
person through whom Amis's literary and linguistic humor could cred-
ibly be conveyed,[5] and even Max Hunter, the author of the poem "To
a Child Born without Limbs," with its nastily funny punning on clichés
such as "putting your best foot forward," is presented as a man who
dislikes music and poetry and "having to think about things" (Part 3).
The last reason for the lack in *The Anti-Death League* of stylistic and/
or comic ornament is the most obvious one: the nature of the spy-
thriller itself, which needs to be taken seriously by the less sophisticated
reader, and thus to subordinate style to story.

But simplicity of style is not the same as straightforwardness of narrative presentation. The "spy-thriller" element in *The Anti-Death
League* involves detection within the story (who is the spy who is leak-

ing the secret of Operation Apollo?), and carries with it concealment from the reader, as from those of the characters not in security classification S-1 (what *is* Operation Apollo?). As a result, the apparently clear-cut division of the novel into three parts (roughly corresponding to the three phases of the "lethal node" through which it moves) is counterpointed, on the spy level of the story, by the use of indirection, unobvious clues, and even red herrings (Dr. Best the largest of these) in the first two parts, followed by an unduly expository revelation of plot secrets in Part 3. The novel therefore requires, as well as repays, rereading, the first reading tending to concentrate on the mystery of atmosphere and event, the second on the deeper enigma that underlies them: the enigma of life and death which the different characters variously try to face and comprehend. Though it is this essential enigma which the opening of the novel, in uncharacteristically blank fashion, presents, and this which gives the novel its thematic importance, later developments—the "security plot" relating to Captain Leonard, Dr. Best, and the nature and purpose of Operation Apollo—tend to engross the reader's interest and involve him in detective operations of his own; so much so that one wonders whether Amis was well advised to create such an elaborate special mechanism to convey a general metaphysical theme.

Indeed, it is arguable whether the mechanism really does convey— rather than merely accompany—the theme. There is, after all, a degree of difference between the deaths likely to ensue from Operation Apollo (a human plan to spread a kind of hydrophobia among Chinese soldiers), and the various deaths—attributable, it is advanced, to the motiveless malignity of God—which actually occur in the novel: the despatch-rider crushed under a lorry, Corporal Fawkes dead of meningitis, the visiting lecturer (L. S. Caton's last bow!) killed by a stray bullet,[6] Major Ayscue's Alsatian bitch Nancy run over by a lorry. That Amis was aware of a problem here is suggested by the fact that, in Part 2, Captain Max Hunter declares that Operation Apollo is not "an analogy" for the prevalence of death in the world which so worries Churchill or for the likelihood of death by breast cancer of his lover Catherine Casement, the particular situation which finally drives him over the edge of brooding into neurosis.

That the two types of death are nevertheless allowed to coexist and even to seem to blur into one another may be explained as no more than authorial self-indulgence: a wish to combine two types of story in one book, to emulate the elaborate but soluble obscurities of a Len

Deighton while exploring the insoluble human situation. More fruit-fully, the fact that the invention of an operation like "Apollo" entailed of necessity a military ambience (something Amis clearly enjoys build-ing up for its own sake) may have seemed to offer him just that imper-sonal sort of background against which the existence of death could be most bleakly demonstrated. In the words of Captain Ross-Donaldson (whose fondness for the jargon of military science conceals his real importance in the "security plot"), the existence of an "Anti-Death League" threatens to subvert the purpose of Operation Apollo, since the job of the military is to be "pro-death" (Part 2). In that sense, those engaged on the operation could conceivably be seen as functioning as the agents of a cruel God.

Whatever the reasons for Amis's "ambitious" fusion of diverse ele-ments, the result is a novel which considerably extends his technical and philosophical range without being entirely successful as a study of death. But given its presentation of a world in which deaths occur, whether at random or otherwise, in which a barbarous plan like Oper-ation Apollo seems necessary, and in which "ignorant armies clash by night," perhaps the most satisfactory way of regarding it is as a rec-ommendation of the precarious but vital importance of some other words from Matthew Arnold's "Dover Beach"—his injunction "Ah love! let us be true / To one another." If death, the "lethal node" of Churchill's obsessive imagination, broods over the novel, it is love—whether expressed sexually, through friendship and loyalty, or through a devotion to music—which enables a lucky few to live under its shadow, and to emerge from it.

The novel's quietly sinister, slightly Kafkaesque opening, in which things and people are presented generically, rather than specifically ("a girl," "a metalled pathway"), seems deliberately contrived to exclude coziness—there is brightness but no feeling of warmth—and to suggest an inescapable universality in the images of menace and unease it presents: stark light and deep shadow, a black cat stalking a nesting bird, a "tower-like structure," the noise of a low-flying plane, a lionlike but also frighteningly devillike statue later revealed as the work of a paranoiac who went totally mad after finishing it.

It is against this bizarre but appropriate background—the landscape of Dr. Best's mental hospital—that James Churchill sees Catherine Casement and instantaneously falls in love with her: she is recovering from a nervous breakdown, his growing obsession with the omnipres-ence of death drives him to a breakdown near the end of the novel, and each when in need profits from the sanity and love of the other.

Amis's hostility to the psychiatrist Dr. Best is evident throughout: he is described as grotesque-looking, it is his decision that allows the statue to be "our mascot," he cannot accept anything obvious in his patients as genuine, he masks a seamy sexual opportunism under the guise of professional inquiry, he is rejected by the otherwise all-encompassing Lucy Hazell, and he finally goes mad himself, in a passage which sounds like a cross between a stuck phonograph record and the ravings of an unmasked James Bond villain with delusions of master-spyhood. Yet the presence in the novel of the mental hospital he operates has the force of a symbol: the ever-present threat of madness that lurks behind human life, pouncing when life's nastinesses (seen by Churchill and by Max Hunter as the malevolence of God) are looked at too squarely and overcome the ability of man's philosophical or theological systems, or his courage, to outface them.

The point at which the eyes of Churchill and Catherine first meet is described in a way which is very important for the novel as a whole. It exactly coincides with the passing over their heads of the low-flying plane: "Just when the girl turned and looked at the tall young man it was as if the sun went out for an instant. He flinched and drew in his breath almost with a cry." This effect is repeated, significantly modified, when they see each other again after Churchill's visit to Max Hunter (recovering from what sounds like a bout of delirium tremens) and Catherine's interview with Dr. Best in which he sends her out to face the pressures of the world again: "Churchill felt a shock, as if the aircraft had again passed between him and the sun." The two passages, taken together, suggest that love and "the shadow of death" coincide, that love brings vulnerability, that the perception of love and the perception of death are of equal sharpness; and, perhaps most importantly, that they coexist and thus may have equal significance. Just as different views of death, and reactions to it, exist within the novel, so throughout there are sequential and sometimes simultaneous juxtapositions of bad and good events. Such juxtapositions convey the irony of life, but also its mystery.

For Churchill the ironies, or mysteries, of juxtaposition resolve themselves into an "overall evil pattern." His love for Catherine sharpens his response to the external world, making him take "its and her joint existence as a signal, almost a guarantee, that the real joyful life existed somewhere." This, and his noticing "a stream splashing down among the rocks,"[7] recalls the poignant hopefulness of *Lucky Jim*. But immediately afterwards a pleasant young despatch-rider, bringing a superfluous message for Captain Leonard, is run over by a lorry. For Moti

Naidu, the Indian officer who represents in the novel the detachment of wisdom and the dignity of not whining at unpleasant events, this event "simply happened," but for Churchill it begins his brooding on life's "meaning": "Imagine dying delivering this." By the end of Part 1, his requited love for Catherine has made unpleasantness fade into "dead facts, infinitely distant"; but their romantic, sexy idyll in the country in Part 2 concludes with Churchill's discovery of a lump on Catherine's breast (one meaning of the term "lethal node"), which is later confirmed as cancer.

To have the malevolence of God—as he sees it—brought so close to home gradually drives Churchill deeper into "a self-sealing pocket of fear and helplessness" (Part 3) touched by what can only be called halfbaked self-pity: certainly his statement that "if there were no such thing as death the whole human race could be very happy" reminds one that he is young rather than reinforces the reasonableness of his hostility to God. To the quality of such a remark the sober exhortations of Naidu—leave God out of it, accept the human responsibility to make things "less bad," "We must all try to become men"—seem the necessary answer, but in the event Churchill is rescued not by resources within himself but by the understanding and greater courage of Catherine; and also by her revelation that Operation Apollo has been canceled. Catherine's description suggests that, in calling off such an evil plan, men (who invented it) have proved themselves superior to God; but one is hardly convinced by this reasoning. Rather, the plan's genuine evil has been intended to frighten off a Chinese invasion and has succeeded in doing so, due to the deliberate use by the War Office of the keen but incompetent Brian Leonard as security officer. It is Deering, Leonard's vulgar-minded batman, who has been the spy all along, not Dr. Best, suspected not only by Leonard but by the reader, led astray by Amis's sudden change of perspective at the end of Part 2, where, having escaped the sweeps of "Exercise Nabob," "Dr. Best watched it go."

The idealistic Churchill may be hostile to God, but his passive acceptance of suffering, by slow self-extinction, alongside and even on behalf of Catherine has a contradictorily Christ-like quality. More positive action against God is taken by the sybaritic, likable homosexual Max Hunter, whose panache is reminiscent of Julian Ormerod in *Take a Girl like You*. He is the author of the bitter poem which so upsets the gaunt, conscientious chaplain, Max Ayscue, and the death which provokes him is the second one to occur in the novel, that of Corporal

Fawkes—an indirect provocation, since that death puts out of his reach the object of his affections, Fawkes's close friend Signalman Pearce. Upset both by the disappointment of his hopes and by the "disastrous" strength of the love which has inspired them, Hunter posts the notice proclaiming the formation of the "Anti-Death League,"[8] which is aimed at uniting all those who hate the kind of pointless, cruel deaths detailed in his examples. Concern over Catherine's cancer prompts him to a further futile gesture, the pulverization of St. Jerome's Priory with an atomic rifle. (St. Jerome produced the Vulgate, so the futile gesture has a symbolic appropriateness.) The explosion immediately follows (and interrupts) an angry outburst by Churchill to Catherine— "I want to do something that'll show—"—so that it functions as a vicarious fulfillment of Churchill's wish to protest. Hunter's actions have a raging, frustrated decency about them. "To do nothing," he tells the efficient civilian security man Jagger, "would be simply offensive." Their acceptability in the novel lies precisely in their thoughtlessness, their not being proffered as intellectual solutions of anything.

As sympathetic as Max Hunter, but in a very different way, is Major Ayscue, the worried, thoughtful, music-loving chaplain. Ayscue (askew?) is almost a Graham Greene character, a priest who feels deeply all the deaths in the novel, but who because of his own religious doubts thinks himself inadequate to offer effective consolation or explanation. It is hard (without abandoning all trust in the shrewdness of theological selection boards) to credit his original reason for joining the church: to subvert a barbarous God from the inside. It is easier to accept his later shift of feeling: whether or not God exists, the human wish to believe in His benevolence is not ignoble. He ministers conscientiously to this "conspiracy" of belief because, basically, he wants to share it, and in the complex final scene in which the Trio Sonata by "Thomas Roughead,"[9] discovered by him in Lucy Hazell's library, has its first performance, the contrast between his sincerely meant rhetoric (man's music as a gift of God and an expression of "God's glory") and his inner doubts is movingly conveyed.

There is much irony in this closing scene, but much mystery, too. The mystical revelation of "somebody . . . at the other end of the telephone" that Ayscue receives as he prays after his sermon for Catherine's complete recovery seems to promise "a joy so enormous that it justified everything"; yet as the sonata begins, his dog, tied up outside, breaks free and is run over by a lorry. The "accidental" death balances that of the despatch rider at the beginning and seems a nasty divine

joke to answer the plea of Roughead's anthem "Lord, Protect Thou
Thy Servants." Yet, earlier in the same scene, Ayscue has had a secular
revelation, that music is "the true embodiment of the unaided and self-
constituted human spirit, the final proof of the non-existence of God."
Nancy, his dog, has broken free because "music had always had a bad
effect on her." What, then, has killed her: God's dubious "glory," a
dead man's rediscovered music, or the steering of a lorry which "failed
to respond" to the driver's attempt to avoid her? The physical ending
of the novel is bleak, but its philosophy is wisely left open-ended, in
view of the inscrutability of the subject.

If there is any conclusion to the problem of death in *The Anti-Death
League* it is perhaps expressed, in his blank despair, by James Churchill: "There's nothing to say, except about this thing. And there's nothing
to say about that." It is a view which resembles that expressed by Philip
Larkin in his roughly contemporaneous poem about death, "Nothing
to be Said":

> And saying so [that "life is slow dying"] to some
> Means nothing; others it leaves
> Nothing to be said.[10]

If there is any comparatively unshadowed happiness in the novel, it is
found by those who do not worry themselves too much about the
metaphysics of existence: the kindly, promiscuous Lucy Hazell, with
her "maison à une fille" which eases the tensions of so many at the
camp, and the military romantic Brian Leonard, with his touching
devotion to his adopted regiment "the Sailors" (who sound like
Waugh's "Halberdiers" in *Sword of Honour*) and his fierce, outsider's
attachment to such "traditions" as the tiny, carefully ironed white cot-
ton gloves made not to be worn but to be carried into the officers' mess.
His serious wooing of Lucy Hazell is virtually an inversion of Patrick's
seduction of Jenny, and at the end, as they sit together at the Roughead
concert, it seems likely that he will have "all of her" to himself, a consolation prize for the disappointment of his efforts as a security officer
and for the humiliating revelation (by Ross-Donaldson) that he was
expected to fail to keep the secrets of Operation Apollo from the
Chinese. It is significant of Amis's involvement with the military context of his serious spy-story that he should have declared, in 1974:
"Brian is my favourite character in the book, because of his naïvety.
He is a chivalrous fool."[11] For all its conscientious, wide-ranging, vexed

and often moving presentation of last things, *The Anti-Death League* extends tolerance also to those who place first things first: duty, friendship, love.

II The Green Man (1969)

Though *The Green Man* issues from the same preoccupation with God, death, and evil as *The Anti-Death League*, Amis's second "genre" novel published under his own name is very different in feeling from its predecessor. In *The Anti-Death League* Amis holds himself at some distance from his characters, and the hermetic world of a security-conscious army camp is well rendered by the novel's detached, rather clinical manner, and by the noticeable lack of precise indications of place. That world, however, obeys the ordinary rules of "reality": God and Evil exist in it, but are perceived by their effects— a "node" of apparently fateful happenings which represents the thickening, or junction, of the separate, apparently random paths and events of which life usually seems composed.

Another meaning of *The Anti-Death League's* term "node" is "the point where a planet's orbit crosses the ecliptic," the apparent path of the sun. For this the aptest literary equivalent is T. S. Eliot's notion, in *Four Quartets,* of "the intersection of the timeless with time." This intersection occurs in *The Green Man* in an absolutely literal way: the novel is a ghost story, in which not only the evil principle appears, in the form of the seventeenth-century "wizard"[12] Dr. Thomas Underhill, who lived in the house before it became a hotel, but also God himself, fundamentally good but embodied in the disturbing form of "a young, well-dressed, sort of after-shave lotion kind of man."[13] When, in Part 4, "the young man" materializes, time and "all molecular motion" stop for a period of exactly twenty-four minutes. The establishment of this precise interval by the hero (for Maurice Allington is morally central to the novel, not merely the narrator of its events) is typical of the detailed realism Amis employs. In part, in standard ghost-story fashion, this realism acts as the necessary foil for the supernatural happenings; but its more important purpose is to insist, by anchoring these to a definite physical world, on their own actuality, and on their vital significance for Allington himself.

The physical existence of the novel's setting is announced right at the beginning by a device which crosses the boundary between fiction and contemporary fact: the description of Allington's hotel, The Green

Man, in terms of an exact copy of an entry in the British *Good Food Guide*, complete with specimen dishes, prices, and a list of satisfied clients, all of them actual people,[14] one of them Amis's good friend and political ally, the journalist Bernard Levin. It is perhaps a slightly self-indulgent private joke, but it works in establishing Allington as a "real" hotelier, as does his own reference to the actual John Fothergill who described his inn, the Spread Eagle at Thame (near Oxford), in his book *An Innkeeper's Diary*. The "entry" also allows Amis to mention, casually, the existence of a ghost. Amis's attitude to The Green Man's geographical location is equally "factual," not only through his references to Stevenage, Royston, Baldock, and Cambridge, but in his placing of the imaginary village of "Fareham"—the "place of fear" of the fictional story—equidistant from the two real villages of Sandon and Mill End.[15] Similarly, later on, Amis places his imaginary "St. Matthew's College" just between the real St. Catharine's College and the corner of Silver Street in Cambridge.

The action of the novel is presented entirely from the point of view of Maurice Allington, who narrates it, retrospectively, in an idiosyncratic style crackling with prejudices. Many individual paragraphs are like mini-essays: on his Siamese cat, Victor Hugo, who dies heroically at the end, on his jaundiced attitude to food (shared by Amis, who also has a Siamese cat),[16] on the dreariness of rural peasant life, on the "puny and piffling art" of novelists, on the absurdities of radical student Cambridge in the 1960s. For Allington, only a "tiny proportion of humanity" is "more entertaining than bad television," and at fifty-three he finds himself haunted by the fear of personal extinction, which perhaps explains his rather joyless and theoretical pursuit of sex with Diana Maybury, the "blonde, full breasted" wife of his doctor. This is conveyed with a typically Amisian turn of sardonic wit in Part 2: "I am too old a hand to be put off pleasure by even the certain prospect of not enjoying it. What will have been, will have been." Allington prefers fantasizing about sex, and having it, to talking to the real women who are its objects: his second wife, Joyce (whose "listlessness" recalls Jean Lewis), fails to interest him as a person, and even his lust for Diana is almost put out of its stride when, like a latter-day Margaret Peel, she quotes the opening of Langland's *Piers Plowman* before willingly surrendering to him in a secluded hollow. It is, perhaps, not surprising that when he finally achieves (in Part 4) his perverse ambition of getting both Joyce and Diana into bed with him, they turn to each other and exclude him. But by this time he hardly cares, since his involvement with Dr. Underhill has come to engross him, offering as it does—along with its very real menace—possible evidence of "some form of survival after death" and thus the excitement, in contrast with everything else around him, of "something of which the end was unforeseeable" (Part 3).

Allington's excessive drinking and his inability to relate well even to his family, including Amy, his thirteen-year-old daughter by his previous marriage, prevent him from being an easily likable character; but he is not an unsympathetic one, partly because his narration draws the reader into his point of view, partly because his fear of death and his feelings of guilt and inadequacy render him responsive to the ghosts, the sinister leaflike rustlings, and the seductive approaches of Dr. Underhill which the novel presents as negative aspects of an unseen dimension of the spirit. As if to outface a sceptical reader, Amis makes Allington's responsiveness a function of his alcoholism: he suffers from "jactitation" (twitching of the limbs); he suffers unpleasant and lengthy "hypnagogic hallucinations," out of which comes his first horrified vision of the huge, lumbering tree shape after which his hotel is perhaps named; he has a habit of dangerous driving which leads in Part 4 to a bad accident; and he tends to do things without being aware of them, so that his first interview with Dr. Underhill has for "evidence" only the disjointed notes he discovers afterwards. But though the tiny scarlet and green bird which so terrifies him on its first appearance ("I picked up my towel, rolled it into a ball and screamed into it for perhaps two minutes") is offered as a symptom of delirium tremens, the hosts of them which attack him in Part 4 are part of the pornographic phantasm unleashed by Dr. Underhill at their final midnight rendezvous.

The vividness of that supernatural scene, and the immediacy with which the many other such incidents in the novel are presented, make it impossible to disbelieve them. "It all really happens," Amis declared in 1975; "none of what is recounted happens only in the hero's mind."[17] Lucy, Allington's daughter-in-law, to whom he is initially shown as hostile but whom he gradually comes to like, is the only other person in the novel who even admits the possible reality of ghosts; but, rationalistically, she requires, as confirmation, the sharing of Allington's experiences by someone else. To the two most frightening scenes in the book Amis adds this rational confirmation by involving Allington's daughter Amy. Underhill is reputed to have murdered his wife, and in Part 3 Allington, seeing the light of the present out of one window of

The Green Man and the moonlit dark of the past from another, unwillingly witnesses its reenactment: the pursuit of the wife by Underhill's familiar—an immense, ungainly Frankenstein's monster made of wood, twigs, and rotting leaves—followed, out of sight, by a loud clear screaming and "a wailing or an unsteady hooting . . . like a high wind, through trees." Amy hears the noises but is unaware of the darkness, the slip backwards in time.

In the climactic scene, at the end of Part 4, the past enters the present. Underhill's papers, discovered at "All Saint's College," Cambridge (their style is an Amisian tour-de-force of seventeenth-century pastiche), have obscurely indicated his search for a means of self-perpetuation, but have also fully revealed his uses of the occult for the purpose of terrifying, then seducing young village girls. Now, unable to satisfy his desires physically, he entices Amy to walk out of the house and sends "the green man" to kill her: she has reached the right age to interest him, and at last Allington realizes why Underhill has been trying, across the centuries, to attract his attention. The reader also realizes why Allington has been an apt subject for his wiles: he has felt responsible (though unnecessarily) for his own first wife's death, and he has himself resembled Underhill in being as experimenter, a manipulator of women for merely sexual ends. Nor is it by accident that Allington's various perceptions of the lurking presence of the "green man" have usually occurred after scenes of sexual indulgence: Underhill is a kind of supernatural voyeur. By throwing the cold, silver emblem of the green man, found by Allington in Underhill's coffin, back where it belongs, Allington causes the monster to disintegrate with "a drawn-out, diminishing howl of inhuman pain and rage"; in human terms, he has accepted responsibility for his daughter and has saved her life. At the end of the novel their new closeness is shown by her asking her father to turn off her television set. Loneliness caused by his neglect has conditioned her to watch anything on it, however dull or trivial; now she no longer needs to. Allington's previous unwillingness to spend any time talking to Joyce causes her finally to leave him; with Amy he seems unlikely to repeat this mistake.

Part of Allington's interest in Underhill comes from an "affinity" in selfishness which at the end he renounces, forcing the local "modernist" clergyman (who languidly deprecates such "religious mumbojumbo") to exorcise both the last, scattered fragments of the green man and Underhill's grave. Allington refuses Underhill's final, tempting offer, whispered pleadingly during the exorcism service, "I'll teach you

peace of mind." The wish for such peace of mind is the other reason
he has "come in search" of Underhill: he longs for some proof of
human immortality to replace a fear of death so strong that he cannot
imagine why it does not engross everyone's thoughts, a fear accompanied by "a bit of anger and hatred and indignation perhaps, and loathing and revulsion, and grief, I suppose, and despair" (Part 2). He no
longer really needs this peace of mind from Underhill—or rather, he
is able to live without it—because of the visit he has had in Part 3 from
God himself, in the guise of an urbane, silky-haired young man who
leaves him "a little keepsake"—a silver crucifix which he later uses to
repel Underhill's phantasms—and answers his question about an after-
life with what amounts to a yes: "You'll never be free of me, while this
lot lasts." "This lot" is the scheme of things as presently constituted, a
scheme which includes human free will, and denies foreknowledge to
God. Nor is God malicious: such arbitrary cruelties as occur are simply
part of a system with which God, its author, cannot now interfere. (The
scheme of things also includes evil: as Milton almost realized, Satan is
"a piece of God.")

These pronouncements of Amis's God have a proper obscurity and
are only equivocally comforting, but in being an attempt at a synthesis
they represent an advance on the various positions indicated in *The
Anti-Death League;* what is suggested in *The Green Man* is that an
interest in death (one aspect of God) is an interest in all God's aspects,
the nature of which (the divine pattern behind the apparent random-
ness of events) is kept hidden in order to stimulate faith. But one definite statement the "young man" does make, in accordance with traditionalist views of the Church which Amis expressed in the 1970
postscript to his essay "On Christ's Nature": God exists, and is an eternal spirit, not the contemporary inciter of opposition to repressive
right-wing regimes, the "sort of suburban Mao Tse-tung" he is made
out to be by the "lefty" rector of Fareham, Tom Rodney Sonnenschein,
who thinks the idea of immortality unnecessary in a Welfare State and
is one of Amis's most devastating, if perhaps exaggerated (does he have
to be homosexual as well?), portraits of "trendiness."[18]

Behind Amis's use of the ghost-story form in *The Green Man* lies
the influence of M. R. James, whose *Ghost Stories of an Antiquary*
(1904) and later volumes were published in a Collected Edition in
1931.[19] Dr. Underhill, who frightens village girls with apparitions,
strongly resembles the evil Karswell in "Casting the Runes," and
Underhill's green familiar may be Amis's attempt to visualize the

unknown "something" which terrifies John Harrington to death.[20] A wind (cf. Amis's "movement in the grass") and a pursuing shape flit eerily through "Oh, Whistle, and I'll Come to You, My Lad," and "The Stalls of Barchester Cathedral" employs the motif of dusty personal papers discovered in a college library. But to suggest the place of Amis's novel in a literary tradition in no way reduces its independent capacity to frighten, and Amis's introduction of God not only extends the scope of the ghost-story genre but formally encapsulates a grey area of human experience within a larger concern with life and eternity.

Commenting on *The Green Man*, Amis said in 1975 that "I think it should be taken very seriously; I took it very seriously indeed."[21] Tight, gripping, and totally without defensive ironies, *The Green Man* is one of Amis's best novels; paradoxically, perhaps, the ghost-story genre, which can be seen as "only fiction" but by its nature implies a dimension beyond the visible world, allows him to speak more freely, and more deeply, about God, death, and human life than he has often managed to do in nongeneric novels. Amis's seriousness is evident in the fine, cumulative rhythms of the penultimate paragraph, which convey powerfully Maurice Allington's sense of the limitations of self-hood, and substitute for the fear of bodily extinction what is almost a longing for the escape from personality which death, in due time, will bring:

Death was my only means of getting away for good from this body and all its pseudo-symptoms of disease and fear [. . .] from attending to my own thoughts and from counting in thousands to smother them and from my face in the glass. He had said I would never be free of him as long as the world lasted, and I believed him, but when I died I would be free of Maurice Allington for longer than that.

CHAPTER 6

Alternate Worlds of Youth

PART of Amis's attraction to the "genre" novel is related to its ability, unlike the modern "high-brow" novel, to cater to "the child and adolescent parts of the reader of serious fiction":[1] the desire to be horrified, to be thrilled, to be diverted. He has praised Dickens for his ability to satisfy such interests in a way impossible, he feels, in the twentieth century, with its division of the novel into "separate little streams." From early on, actual children have played a small but quite important part in Amis's novels: John Lewis tells stories to his daughter Eira, Garnet Bowen is pursued by the hypothetical questions of his young sons ("If two tigers jumped on a blue whale, could they kill it?"), Roger Micheldene's self-esteem is wounded when Arthur Bang wins at Scrabble; and Jenny Bunn's professional life is concerned with squabbling primary-school children. It is thus no great surprise to find that, in the 1970s, Amis has combined the "genre" novel with the study of an adolescent and a child, respectively: Peter Furneaux in *The Riverside Villas Murder* (1973) and Hubert Anvil in *The Alteration* (1976).

To some extent, given the increasing gloom registered by his "adult" novels from *The Anti-Death League* on through his three nongeneric novels of the 1970s, Amis's contemplation of childhood and adolescence is an escape into simpler and more innocent emotions, into a time when life is, in Philip Larkin's words, "a joyous shot at how things ought to be."[2] Both novels, however, are sufficiently influenced by the pessimism of later middle age to show this innocence at just the moment when it encounters the pressures (atypical ones, admittedly) of the adult world: at the end of their respective novels, neither Peter nor Hubert will ever be the same again. Thus, as with *The Anti-Death League* and *The Green Man*, Amis uses his "genre" novels of the 1970s as vehicles for embodying important themes. *The Riverside Villas Murder* has, too, a particularly interesting schematic link with *The Green Man*, whose perspective it reverses. At the end of *The Green Man*, Maurice Allington recognizes and responds to the cool, loving competence of his thirteen-year-old daughter Amy, who emerges from her obscure child-object status to look after him when his wife leaves. In *The Riverside Villas Murder* it is her viewpoint that takes over, transferred into a fourteen-year-old boy whose situation and personality suggest the young Amis as much as Amy's name resembles his.

I   The Riverside Villas Murder *(1973)*

The Riverside Villas Murder kills a number of birds with one stone; or rather, with the sawn-off Condor glider which the beautiful Mrs. Trevelyan uses to kill her former lover, Christopher Inman. It is a detective story, fully equipped with suspects, alibis, clues, red herrings, and concealed trains of thought, and it aims to fulfill what is for Colonel Manton, its chief detective, "the whole raison d'être of a murder story": namely, "to trick the reader" (Ch. 10).[3] Since, however, it is also a detective story by a literary *aficionado,* it makes lighthearted fun out of the conventions of the form, as when Manton irritates the stolid Inspector Cox by his discussion of dull and less dull murder methods (Ch. 6), and when, at various points, he sends Detective-Constable Barrett, an early product of the new Police College at Hendon, off on searches for evidence which he knows (and says) will prove futile. And within the story there are allusions, open or covert, to other detective stories: in Chapter 12 Manton appears dressed like "a bookie thinly disguised as Sherlock Holmes," and when, near the end, Mrs. Trevelyan is inexorably pointed by Manton in the direction of the "decent thing" (to leave a signed confession and then kill herself, in order not to involve Peter), Amis may well be thinking of the conclusion of Dorothy L. Sayers's *The Unpleasantness at the Bellona Club* (1928).

Considered simply as a detective story, the novel is ingenious and enjoyable, and its murder, prompted by sexual hypocrisy (Inman has threatened to tell Mrs. Trevelyan's husband about the liaison), satisfies the criterion laid down by George Orwell in 1946: "crimes as serious as murder should have strong emotions behind them."[4] The detective story is also an appropriate genre in which to cast a novel using an adolescent hero, since the "boy-detective" is often one of its elements; Peter Furneaux proves both an observant helper of Colonel Manton and a shrewd, independent solver of the mystery. But the novel's deeper attraction lies in the rich nostalgia of its atmospheric details: it offers to the reader the evocation of a period, and for Amis himself, who grew up in that period, it is a celebration of his own adolescent interests and a memory of the place in which they occupied him. More obviously than in any other of his novels, fictional story rides on a thick substratum of recalled personal fact and feeling.

The year of the novel's action is 1936, precisely indicated in Chapter 1 by a reference to the execution of Dr. Buck Ruxton, the murderer, and in Chapter 9, which records the death of "a schoolmaster called M. R. James."[5] Peter, in 1936, is fourteen, as was Amis, and the school he attends is given a name, "Blackfriars Grammar," which virtually identifies it with Amis's City of London School beside Blackfriars Bridge. The 1930s atmosphere is built up, generally, by references to "the wireless," Peter's use of "Anzora" (which preceded Brylcreem as a hair-dressing) and his wearing of that newish phenomenon, a "collar-attached shirt"; by the mention of Croydon Aerodrome nearby, from which the aerial circumnavigations of the era originated, of film stars of the period —Madeleine Carroll, Ginger Rogers—and of the popular dance bands favored by Peter: Ambrose and His Orchestra, Troise and His Mandoliers. Peter is also awakening to sex: Marie Stopes has just published *Change of Life in Men and Women*, and Peter catches Daphne Hodgson reading a near contemporary best-seller, Margaret Kennedy's *The Constant Nymph* (1924).

Another best-seller, Warwick Deeping's *Sorrell and Son* (1925), which Amis read fairly early in his life,[6] influences the way in which he presents the relationship ("old boy" and "Dad") between Peter (an only child) and his father, Captain Furneaux, R.F.C.,[7] whose right arm has apparently been injured in a wartime flying accident in Mesopotamia (Captain Sorrell, father of Kit, won the Military Cross). For much of the time, Peter's father, an estate agent's representative, treats him in a lower-middle-class, pettily repressive way: criticizing his reading of adventure stories in the *Wizard*, objecting to his tastes in music, both jazz and classical, making it difficult for Peter to indulge in "self-abuse" while in the bath. All these elements, together with his "beaky nosed, squarish" build, his passion for tennis, and his professed liking for the music of Sir Arthur Sullivan, cause him to resemble the man whom Amis described in 1967 in his essay "A Memoir of My Father."[8] Despite his father's small tyrannies (in which he does not resemble Warwick Deeping's devoted Stephen Sorrell), Peter likes him, though his trust is strained after Inman's veiled accusations at the tennis-club "flannel dance," and later, more upsettingly, when his father is under suspicion of Inman's murder. Peter's uncertainty—"I don't see," he worries in Chapter 9, "how in this world anyone can ever say they're

sure they know anyone"—is part of his growing up; but when he
finally learns his father's secret (Furneaux was injured in a car crash,
and was never a flyer), their mutual affection is expressed in the open
emotional terms that mark so many of the utterances of *Sorrell and
Son*. Furneaux's eventual honesty makes him, in his son's eyes, "a good
father"; Peter is—though his more embarrassed father quickly chokes
off his own words—"the best son."

Apart from Captain Furneaux, the most important adult male in the
novel is Colonel Manton, the Acting Chief Constable who takes charge
of the investigation and brings wit and imagination to bear on it. He,
too, is treated in a rather "period" way. Genial and sardonic, a real
war hero with an M.C. and a D.S.O., he is one of Amis's most intrigu-
ing and likable characters, despite his exact use to Constable Barrett
(Ch. 2) of the phrase Welch uses to Jim Dixon: "We'll go down in my
car"—a joke the reader is no doubt meant to recognize. Various hints,
including Manton's playfully severe style of talking to Barrett, indicate
his nature: like Max Hunter in *The Anti-Death League*, he is a sympathetic homosexual, or more precisely, in view of his partiality for
Peter, a pederast, who lives in lonely state, sublimating his forbidden
inclinations in a taste for "shit-hot" jazz piano-playing and records of
Louis Armstrong and Fats Waller (Ch. 10). He has even chosen his
housekeeper for her name: Mrs. Ellington. He comes over as a noble
and rather sad figure, who extends Peter's musical awareness ("Imagine," he comments on Louis Armstrong's playing, "what it must feel
like to be able to do that. Any of it.") but finally renounces the possibility of further friendship in a speech of distinctly old-fashioned reticence: "I now know you know what I am, or what I used to be: a small
enough part of my life at any time, but the smallest part is too much"
(Ch.15). It is because he can make this renunciation himself that Manton expects Mrs. Trevelyan to do so, sparing Peter by her suicide the
stigma of having been "debauched in youth by a murderess" (Ch. 14).

Such is the simple, prewar morality of the adults in *The Riverside
Villas Murder*, and there is no doubt that, in his essential innocence,
Peter deserves to benefit from it. He is good-natured, well mannered,
a credible mixture of naïveté and shrewdness[9] who combines the reading of boys' comics, *Carry On, Jeeves*, and *The War of the Worlds*
with a more precocious interest in Maugham and Aldous Huxley. But
he is by no means ignorant of sex. His fair-haired good looks, which
have attracted various men on the train to and from school and which
attract both Manton and Mrs. Trevelyan, are accompanied by an

instinctive understanding of the response they provoke, and by his own budding desires: if Mrs. Trevelyan does indeed seduce him, it is only because, as he reassures her with remarkably sophisticated, consolatory tact in Chapter 9, he is too inexperienced to seduce her.

The novel's description of Peter's sexual experimentation, before he is educated by the experienced Mrs. Trevelyan, is beautifully managed, and combines delicacy with a sort of cool pragmatism. There is no sordidness in his afternoon sessions of mutual masturbation, "moments of delight," with his friend Reg, which are seen as a preparatory substitute for heterosexual activity: "Going second was better because you were still in the mood, or more so, less good because the one who had been first was not, or not so much, but on balance it was considerably better" (Ch. 7). Peter's attempts to implement the school "Code of Dishonour" by approaching the pretty but vacuous girl next door, Daphne Hodgson, are both funny and touching. Reg, Peter's friend, with his Turban cigarettes and collection of lead soldiers, strongly resembles the "Bobby Bailey" who lived in Norbury Avenue, as described in Amis's recent, and very Betjemanesque poem of that title. Betjemanesque, too, is the very name Daphne Hodgson, and Peter's tentative interest in her has, even if more frankly sexual, something of the romantic aura found in some of John Betjeman's poems of approximately this period: "Pot Pourri from a Surrey Garden," "A Subaltern's Love Song," "North Coast Recollections."[10] The social atmosphere of her family (more vulgar than Peter's), and of the tennis-club "flannel dance" (Chs. 3–4) also recalls a novel published in 1936: Elizabeth Bowen's *The Death of the Heart*, with its sharp central description of provincial Seale-on-Sea and the middle-class denizens of the bungalow Waikiki, who include the adolescent library assistant Daphne Heccomb.

If, at the end of the novel, Peter is able to accost Daphne Hodgson with quiet confidence, it is because of what he has learned, sexually, from Mrs. Trevelyan, who is considerate and kind as well as immoral. Emotionally, Peter's situation is less sure. What he has experienced with Mrs. Trevelyan is more than sex:

. . . the happiness rather surprised him at first, until he realized he had had a sort of glimpse of love. . . . it was like an airman flying over a foreign country without landing there. (Ch. 9)

But such a relationship has no future: Peter is both too young, and too sensible, to be swept away by this "glimpse of love," and in any case his later "shivering" realization that Mrs. Trevelyan is the murderer (Ch. 12) confuses his feelings about her even as it causes him to grow up in other ways, distracting him from his reading and making him realize the difference between fiction and life: "Films and books happened outside you" (Ch. 13). A period of oppressive, thundery weather dramatizes his helpless depression. When, finally, he pursues Mrs. Trevelyan along the river in the darkness, and persuades her to give herself up, his feelings are an obscure blend of shock, pity, protectiveness, and sad realism: it is he, not she, who immediately recognizes the impossibility of an outlaw life together on the South Downs. Whatever he feels for her, and however much he wishes to protect her from the consequences of her actions, he cannot do so, and is too clear-eyed to see them as other than "bad."

The conclusion of the novel leaves Peter's future uneasily open. Colonel Manton tells him: "You're a sane human being and you'll survive all this," which seems probable as we see him talking to Daphne, who is at least nearly his own age. But however premature his emotional development has been with Mrs. Trevelyan—a lover and a murderess—it seems unlikely not to affect him:

Whereas she herself was bound to become a more distant figure as time passed, in a different way those two things that were already hard to separate, what she had done with him and what she had done to Inman, would run into one and draw nearer, like a double cloud coming over the horizon into a blue sky. (Ch. 15)

What seems suggested here is an anticipated, rather than a present, sense of loss, and the later effects of delayed shock; though they will probably not have the destructiveness implied by that other, and far greater, "period" novel of childhood, love and death, L. P. Hartley's The Go-Between (1953). But the passage is ominous, nonetheless; and there is perhaps a touch of irony in the novel's final phrase—"He ran towards her"—as Peter sees his mother (a shadowy figure for most of the novel) as she "emerged into view at the far end of the meadow." A novel published not long before the period of this one, Rosamond Lehmann's Invitation to the Waltz (1932), ends with the oddly similar phrase "She ran into it." But Olivia Curtis, its teenage heroine, is running joyfully to meet the dawn of life; Peter, frightened by its implications, is running for comfort. His theoretical innocence is over.

II   The Alteration *(1976)*

It is no large step, in name, from Peter Furneaux (furnaces) to Hubert Anvil, and *The Riverside Villas Murder* and *The Alteration* share one important element: Amis's concern with the impact of sexual emotion on his young protagonist. In addition, each novel contains a violent murder. But in all other respects they are different. When Peter is being questioned by Colonel Manton (Ch. 10), Manton declines to address him in conventional older-to-younger style, on the grounds that "Master Furneaux doesn't suit you at all. It makes you sound like some disgusting old medieval priest with an enormous white beard." The world of *The Alteration* is one in which formal address is of the essence—Master Morley, Dame Anvil, Officer Redgrave—a neomedieval world in which people know their place, or are taught it. Yet it is also "the year of Our Lord one thousand nine hundred and seventy-six." The "alternate world" of Amis's historical nostalgia has given way to a chilling vision of a totalitarian present expressed in the form technically labeled "Alternate World":[11] that subgenre of Science Fiction which results when a writer revises history and produces a "contemporary" society different, at least in externals, from the one the reader inhabits.

Amis had wanted for some years to write science fiction,[12] but this desire does not of itself account for the existence of *The Alteration*, whose origin Amis explained in an interview published in 1974. Sent some EMI archive material to review for *Records and Recording*, he found himself listening to a record, made in 1906, of the last castrato singer, Alessandro Moreschi— a forty-six-year-old man with a trilling soprano voice. Amis's reaction reveals a clear bias: the singing was "musically very fine . . . but the noise was indescribably depressing." Out of a "jittery depression" which lasted for days (the singer was "no man at all") came the wish to write a novel revolving around the parental consent, the *decision*, which would have resulted in a voice like Moreschi's, since

. . . that decision brings out everything of importance in human life. Your arguments for and against your duty to God, to sing his music. Your duty to art. Sex. Love. Marriage. Children. Fame. Money. Security.[13]

"To alter," as used in the novel, is the official euphemism for "to castrate," and the "Alternate World" form offered Amis the opportunity to investigate, without the bother of historical reconstruction, the situation of a young choirboy whose excellent treble voice exposes him, as in the historical past, to the sacrifice of his sexual powers in the cause of art, and (since "alteration" contains a play on "altar") for the glory of God.

The world—itself an alteration—which Amis has invented in order to make such a decision possible in the twentieth century is introduced, in Chapter 1, by means of a dense layering of initially surprising detail, which is then authenticated, as well as augmented, by the more casual conveying of sparser background information as the novel proceeds. Hence, unlike all Amis's other novels, *The Alteration* begins with a long passage of descriptive exposition: five pages in a style unfamiliarly public and "official"—the style of the old-fashioned third-person narrator, detached and distant. Nevertheless, there is perhaps a particular literary precedent for Amis's juxtaposition, at the start of his novel, of Hubert Anvil's singing and roll-call of a "distinguished assembly": namely, the opening of Ronald Firbank's *The Eccentricities of Cardinal Pirelli* (1926), with its gathering of "the Altamissals, the Villarasas . . . and Catherine, Countess of Constantine" to witness the christening of the Duquesa Dun Eden's "week-old police dog." As Monsignor Silex, the Pontiff's emissary, gazes round at this strange scene, "from the choir-loft a boy's young voice was evoking heaven."[14] Amis's beginning, whose stately rhythms recall the opening of another Firbank novel, *Valmouth* (1919), is a sort of "square" version of Firbank's rococo fantasy. Amis, too, has emissaries on a mission from the Pope, two castrati—a "leading singer in secular opera" and the director of the Sistine Choir— to whom he gives the Firbankian names Federicus Mirabilis and Lupigradus Viaventosa.

Hubert Anvil, whom they have come to hear, is the best boy soprano in living memory; he is singing, in St. George's Cathedral Basilica at Coverley (Cowley outside Oxford), at the funeral service of King Stephen III of England. The turning point in history which has led to a monarch so named was located, it transpires, in the sixteenth century; instead of dying young, our Henry VIII's elder brother Prince Arthur remained married to Catherine of Aragon and sired a line of rulers who, with the later assistance of an unelaborated "Holy Expedition" and "Holy Victory," kept England a Catholic country. Europe, too, remained Catholic; instead of fathering the Reformation, Martin Luther blackmailed Rome with the strength of his following and himself obtained the Papacy under the style of Germanian I. (In a deadpan reference to Frederick Rolfe's novel, Amis indicates also that Sir Thomas More became Pope Hadrian VII.) Politically, or, rather, theologically, the present world is divided into a Catholic Europe and its extensive overseas dominions; their traditional enemy, the realm of Islam, headed by the "Sultan-Calif of Turkey"; and "New England," a country smaller than the United States, inhabited by Red Indians and the descendants of "Schismatics" and convicts (including William Shakespeare) exiled from Europe.

It is New England, encountered in the person of its musical, liberal-minded ambassador Cornelius van den Haag, that suggests the possibility of refuge to Hubert when he is (Ch. 5) on the run. What has produced his plight is, essentially, the all-powerfulness in Europe and England of the Catholic Church, the embrace of whose ecclesiastical monopoly is tightened by Amis's device of giving "two aged representatives of the Holy Office" the names Himmler and Beria, and calling the Pope's second-in-command Cardinal Berlinguer.[15] Such types, it is implied, rise to the top in whatever totalitarian organization is available. Such a device is, of course, also funny; as is the presentation of Turner, Gainsborough, and an "excessively traditionalist" David Hockney as religious painters, the turning of Jean-Paul Sartre into a Jesuit and A. J. Ayer into a professor of Dogmatic Theology, and the listing among Hubert Anvil's reading of such transmogrified classics as *St. Lemuel's Travels*, *Lord of the Chalices*, and the Father Bond stories (Ch. 3). But all these instances serve as a means to an end, in cumulatively driving home the pervasive presence of the Church in everyone's life. And if the reader is inclined merely to laugh at Amis's sometimes mischievous, sometimes malicious ingenuity—a laughter which the book's level tone and involving, claustrophobic atmosphere gradually inhibit—he is urged to see his own world from the outside, as itself a fiction produced by an accident of history, by the "Counterfeit World" novel clandestinely read by Hubert and his fellow-choristers in their dormitory.[16] The world of *The Man in the High Castle*, substantially our own, is both amusing and shocking to them, containing as it does *The Origin of Species* and the inventions of a science largely distrusted in theirs.

Hubert Anvil, whose magnificent voice pulls down on his unwitting ten-year-old head the vast weight of religious orthodoxy, is otherwise an entirely normal child, and an extremely likable one. He combines a stolid appearance with a quick intelligence, and a devotion to music with an instinctive response to the rural surroundings of his choir-

school, appropriately called St. Cecilia's. Beneath his genuine devout-
ness, and his pride in his musical skill, one is quickly made to perceive
other elements: an interest in adventure and an independence in form-
ing judgments (both visible in his interest in schismatic New England,
which precedes his meeting with its ambassador), and the first stirrings
of an awareness of sex and of tenderness. One may recognize the latter
in his persevering, friendly approaches to the calf which lives near St.
Cecilia's, whose function in the novel seems to be to suggest the childish vulnerability of Hubert himself. The awareness of sex, precocious,
perhaps, but vital in the novel's scheme of values, is first announced
when Hubert sees Ned the brewer's boy making love to a girl in the
woods. Their excitement transmits itself to Hubert, who recognizes the
importance and pleasure of what they are doing without fully understanding it, and the pastoral surroundings in which the lovemaking
takes place give it a kind of natural rightness that cancels out any
incidental crudity. Even later, when Ned describes to Hubert what he
had been doing (Ch. 4), it is the intense force of this "emotion recollected in tranquillity" that Hubert (and the reader) responds to, rather
than the peasant explicitness of the language Ned uses.

Against these intimations of a wish in Hubert for a full and normal
life, the arguments advanced in Chapter 1 in favor of the "alteration"
which will deprive him of it can carry only theoretical weight. They
are, however, put forward fairly enough, by the castrati from Rome,
and by Hubert's superiors, Abbot Peter Thynne and Father Dilke.
Having created a Europe in which the Catholic Church is a sort of
malign international corporation, Amis nevertheless takes seriously the
genuineness of its religious roots; some men, Thynne and Dilke
included, are almost wholly sincere in identifying the will of the
Church with the will of God, and Thynne particularly is a complex
and sympathetic character, austere but not harsh, concerned for the
glory which will accrue to England if Hubert's voice is surgically preserved yet concerned also for Hubert's welfare, temporal as well as
spiritual. Hubert and his father should feel privileged to bow to the
will of God; but though Thynne admits no alternative to the alteration
itself, he is sure that it should take place in England, with Hubert's
family nearby, not in Rome. If one could imagine an Ayscue (the chaplain in *The Anti-Death League*) fully convinced of the value of his
calling and of the existence of God, Abbot Thynne would be he.

The arguments for and against Hubert's alteration are presented in the first three chapters largely in terms of a career as a superlative and famous singer versus the retention by Hubert of the more ordinary potential to marry and to propagate. (A reference in Chapter 2 to the twentieth-century English boy soprano, Ernest Lough, [17] whose later baritone voice was inferior, is used by the abbot to reinforce the view that Hubert cannot have both.) But the abbot, a celibate, does not reach his decision on this basis, rather as a result of his weighing of Hubert's two musical skills. For Master Morley, his lay composition teacher, Hubert promises to take his place "with Weber, Schumann, even Valeriani"; but this, despite his reluctance to see Hubert altered, he cannot guarantee, whereas Hubert's voice is a present fact and, preserved by surgery, will be a continuing glory—one which, it is indicated, will effectively rule out composing.

The conclusion, it would seem, is hard but clear: "Anvil goes to the surgeon as soon as the formalities are complete." But for the reader the matter is less simple; or rather, his conclusion is a different one. Amis's throwing of a likely career as a good composer into the scale-pan with sex betrays his own bias, but it is one with which the contemporary reader is likely to agree: two good things, especially where one of them is another aspect of music, are better than a single excellent one, which will exclude so much. The element of composition serves a purpose other than to reveal authorial bias, however. A ten-year-old boy, though he is growing aware of sex and romantic love, cannot realistically be shown functioning entirely in relation to them—cannot, that is, fully realize what their loss would mean. But to give up composing in favor of singing is a choice Hubert understands. In Chapter 4 his daring "improvvisazione" deeply impresses Morley, and when his instincts finally drive him to escape (Ch. 5), his conscious decision is shown to be based on what Morley has told him then: alteration will mean "an end to your activities as a composer."

This is not to deny that the wish to lead a normal life is bound up in his resolution. Indeed, Hubert's response to the sight of Ned and his girl is intense enough to drive from his head for a moment the Theme and Variations he has been thinking out; and when, in Chapter 2, he visits the van den Haags' home and meets their blue-eyed, beautiful daughter Hilda (also ten), he realizes that his singing is for her and experiences "bewilderment and a vague but powerful longing." Though more interested in looking after an unhappy child than in listening to Hubert's singing, Hilda is also attracted to him, and utters a

New England phrase which includes the word "Kisakihitin." Eventually, when Hubert's destiny has been decided and the phrase can have only theoretical meaning, she translates it: "I love thee." (Ch. 6).

The force of human emotion—inchoate in Hubert—is made clear to the reader by the affair between Hubert's mother, Margaret, and Father Matthew Lyall, the family chaplain, who, together with Tobias, Hubert's father, must sign the necessary papers giving permission for the alteration. Tobias, a devout if rather stern and unimaginative man, is willing to fulfill his duty to the Church; even when, in Rome (Ch. 4), he meets Viaventosa and Mirabilis, and sees with horror the high-pitched obesity, touched with "queerness," which may be his son's future lot as a physical being, he still sees that duty as unavoidable: "endure it I must." Hubert's mother, though she tries to convince him of the official line that "the love of men and women is not the highest kind of love" (Ch. 3), is instinctively opposed, and her opposition is sharpened after she has slept with Lyall. Lyall, moving from initial bloody-minded resistance to authority to a sense of responsibility for Hubert's welfare based on love for his mother, determines to hinder the will of the Church, and pays for his folly with his life. That the Church, when openly defied, functions like a police state is implied when one of its bureaucrats, Brother Collam Flakerty, to whom Lyall appeals for help, burns the notes of their conversation immediately afterwards (Ch. 4). The fact is underlined when Lyall is interrogated by two officials of the "Secular Arm" dressed in quasi-Nazi uniforms, despatched by the head of the "Holy Office," which has been informed of Lyall's recalcitrance by an overzealous spy in Abbot Thynne's household. (Maliciously, Amis calls the head of the Holy Office "The Lord Stansgate," and his officers Foot and Redgrave.[18]) Finally (Ch. 5), Lyall is found dying from shock and loss of blood; he has been castrated, thus suffering painfully the painless fate he has tried to deflect from Hubert.

Such an occurrence (which horrifies Thynne and Dilke— "Our polity," the latter sincerely believes, "is imperfect but not evil") reflects a harsh light back on what is, at first sight, the high comic moment of *The Alteration*: Hubert's central interview with Pope John XXIV. The journey of Hubert and his father on the diesel "railtrack" across "the Channel Bridge, Sopwith's masterpiece," their slow walk through the grounds of the Vatican and its immense, splendid rooms, culminate in the bathetic *coup-de-théâtre* of a "broad, plumpish man of fifty or more" in a dark suit, who greets "Hubert lad" in broad Yorkshire, and offers him the job of "principal, uh, soprano of our church here." The

Pope himself is tone-deaf, and bluffly contemptuous of "the lingo" and "the local muck"; nevertheless, his aim is to acquire the best of everything for Rome. It should become, he says, "a city fit to make Byzantium look like a mill-town." though, as he explains in a characteristic passage:

"Ee, we don't speak of mere temporal glory. . . . To follow after that would be a sin, and if there's one thing we can't abide at any price it's sin. We think we can safely say that."

The hilarious *pièce de resistance* of his homely style comes when the papal plural is used in his offer to pour tea: "Shall we be mother?" It is difficult to think of such a man (could he be in any way a caricature of Harold Wilson?[19]) as the spider at the center of Mother Church's web, yet he is. It is in exactly this colloquial manner that, in Chapter 6, he decides to scrap his abortive attempts to reduce the expanding population of Europe by putting "Crick's Conductor" in the drinking-water,[20] and instead foment a war with the Turks ("our Abdul") which, fifteen years later, has resulted in "thirty million Christians dead, men, women and children." To a man with such an attitude, the alteration of one English choirboy can mean nothing. And as he plans the war, he reflects with pleasure on the final acquisition of Hubert for Rome, and the discomfiture of Abbot Thynne, who has tried to protest. With genial ruthlessness he reflects on the latter's posting to Madras: "It's a fine city, we hear, though a touch hot in summer."

For Hubert does finally reach Rome, though not by unaided human agency. Chapter 5, which describes his nocturnal escape on horseback from St. Cecilia's (reminiscent of John Wyndham's *The Crysalids*[21]), his journey to London by rail-track, his Dickensian abduction by Jews (who have no civil rights and must wear yellow stars on their sleeves), his period of asylum in the New England embassy and his attempted journey to New England by airship, is an exciting narrative but it leads only to anticlimax and the denial of his hopes. Hubert is suddenly struck by a pain at the base of the abdomen: a testicle has turned over and its blood supply has been cut off. The resultant operation, for bilateral torsion (a rare but possible condition, which may require such surgery[22]), achieves to save Hubert's life just that condition originally proposed to preserve his voice.

Perhaps Amis felt that to allow Hubert to escape unscathed to New England was too easy a solution; in any case, New England society, with its policy of "separation" and its use of alteration for sexual offenders, is itself imperfect. The expedient he chose, though a Hardyesque coincidence and literal "twist of fate," resolves the problem of Hubert in a manner in keeping with the book's somber tone, and avoids both the unacceptability of Hubert's choosing alteration and the horror of its being forced on him. It also conveys, perhaps, a rooted authorial pessimism akin to Philip Larkin's: the novel suggests a choice, but events prove choice an illusion. What happens to Hubert is "what something hidden from us chose." [23] But in the religious world of *The Alteration*, that something may be considered to be God, disposing where man proposes, and answering the petition made to him by Abbot Thynne while Hubert is on the run:

Enter into his heart and mind, O Lord, and send him the desire to return here among those who care for him. Or, if that is not Thy purpose, bring it about in Thine own way that he forsake the path of rebellion and outlawry and be brought at last to serve Thy will. (Ch. 5)

It is a prayer which, since it involves loss, Ayscue's God would have been happy to grant.

The latter part of Chapter 6, which ends with a glimpse of Hubert fifteen years later, involves what seems a deliberate lowering of emotional pressure, a distancing irony which yet carries with it an undertone of regret. The events of "1976" are far in the past, and not all has been loss. Hubert has retained his marvelous voice and is a famous singer at Rome, though as Morley prophesied he no longer composes. When he finishes Valeriani's aria "Che è migliore?" Viaventosa and Mirabilis can answer its question—"Which is better?"—with a choral exchange of mellow pieties—"Deo gratia/Amen"—which round out the story satisfyingly for them. For the reader the answer is not so easy. Hubert Anvil has disappeared in Hubertus Incus, in wig and paint, who can only "imagine" the life of his former fellow-clerk Thomas, now a journalist "with a wife and a child and another on the way." Hubertus Incus, remembering the past, finds it "easiest and best" to say that the blue cross, given him in hospital by Hilda, is "his mother's gift." The poignant story of Dawn Daughter and White Fox, separated by the gods, which Hilda told him when he took refuge at the embassy, has come to stand for their separation, and there will never be "another time" for them to complete as adults the conversations they began as children.

The reader, of course, is at liberty to feel that on one level the elaborately created world of *The Alteration* presents an unlikely— indeed, a nonexistent—story. But on another level it is a powerful and moving parable of the limitations and disappointments of the human condition and of the "alteration" of growing up. Recovering from his operation, Hubert realizes, with a remote sadness, that "he would never fit the pieces together"—the pieces of his own particular puzzle. But the generalization toward which he gropes applies to lives led outside the Alternate World which he inhabits: "Perhaps that was how everyone found themselves going about matters, nothing ever measured or settled or understood, not even when they came to die."[24]

CHAPTER 7

"The Only End of Age"

IN its context in Philip Larkin's poem "Dockery and Son,"[1] "the only end of age" means death, the inevitable end of the line. Of Amis's three remaining novels of the 1970s, which straddle the two "genre" novels treated in Chapter 6, only *Ending Up* shows its characters actually reaching their destination; but the other two, *Girl, 20* and *Jake's Thing,* are so aware of its approach, so concerned with the pursuit of desperate remedies and what may in more than one sense be called last stands, that they fit well under the black umbrella of Larkin's phrase. All three novels derive much of the force of their frustration, anger, and harsh comedy from their author's awareness of the shadow of death, and the first two are among Amis's finest achievements.

I   Girl, 20 *(1971)*

Set in the turn-of-the-1960s world of boutiques, pop groups, the youth-cult, and drug abuse, *Girl, 20* shares with its immediate predecessor, *The Green Man,* a seething, spitting distaste for "with-it" modernity and an underlying sense of the emptiness of life without beliefs. It is not an easy novel to sum up, since its opposed values—broadly speaking, "squareness" and "swingingness"—are undercut by the inconsistency of the two main characters who represent them, but its atmosphere may, with important reservations, be indicated by Yeats's lines in "The Second Coming":

> The best lack all conviction, and the worst
> Are full of passionate intensity.

Girl, 20 (the title refers to the advertisements for flat-sharing which appear in such metropolitan newspapers as the *Evening Standard*) is entirely set in London and its immediate environs, and particular locales are drawn from Amis's own experience. The narrator has a flat in Maida Vale, which was where Amis was living when he wrote *The Anti-Death League,* and the Vandervanes' house, "a reputedly grand establishment on the fringes of the Hertfordshire countryside," is a portrait of Lemmons, the large house beside Hadley Common near Barnet where Amis and his wife lived from the late 1960s until 1976.[2] (The Vandervanes' Cavalier King Charles spaniel, "the Furry Barrel," is based on the Amises' own dog.) The origin of the novel, also, lay in an incident in which Amis himself was involved:

> . . . I was in Tottenham Court Road trying to get a taxi. A taxi swept past a small brown man and stopped for me. I thought, wouldn't it be funny if I said to the driver, "You racialist." Wait a second: not me, another man. And it would be better if there were a cock-hungry girl with him at the time, who wouldn't like him doing it—who wanted him to climb into the cab and shut up. Which leads you to a man of liberal sentiments who needs a young and awful girl. Which makes him a trendy Lefty.[3]

This scene, so fictionalized, occurs at the end of Chapter 4, by which time the "trendy Lefty," the fifty-three-year-old conductor Sir Roy Vandervane, has emerged as by no means wholly dislikable, despite his marital and parental irresponsibility and his espousal of fashionable left-wing causes. Sylvia Meers, however, Vandervane's mistress and the "girl, 20" (actually seventeen) of the story, is and remains "awful"; the term used to sum up her attitudes and behavior is "moral vandalism," and she comes perhaps nearer to having no redeeming feature than any other character in Amis's work. To the "small brown man" Amis makes vicarious amends elsewhere: it is one of the novel's pleasanter ironies that the only character who combines decisiveness and old-fashioned human (and moral) concern is the young West Indian writer Gilbert Alexander—despite his being the author of a novel, or rather "my *London Suite* in three movements and three colours," subsidized by the Arts Council.[4]

Perhaps surprisingly, in view of his own increasingly traditionalist attitudes as displayed from the essay "Why Lucky Jim Turned Right" (1967) onward, Amis chose not to present his material in some kind of authorial third person, but by means of a first-person narrator who, in that his prime function is to tell someone else's story rather than his own, differs radically from Amis's earlier first-person narrators, John Lewis and Maurice Allington. In fact, Douglas Yandell in some ways resembles the narrator of Anthony Powell's sequence *The Music of Time:*[5] he observes, reports on, and is confided in about the infatuation of Sir Roy Vandervane for a girl younger than Roy's daughter, while his own life and relationships appear, as it were, in the margin. This method has results more complex than the presumably greater acceptability to the reader of the hostility toward youth displayed by a man of thirty-three (rather than by a "reactionary" author of nearly fifty). The foreground of the novel is occupied by a situation from which one element of sympathy is deliberately withheld (Amis's method ensures that there can be no scene showing Roy and Sylvia alone), but at the same time acceptance of the narrator as an unbiased observer and final judge is weakened by his less than satisfactory handling of his part-time relationship with Vivienne Copes, his waverings between personal loyalty to Roy and disapproval of his behavior, and by the comments— however malicious in intention or grossly overstated some of them are—made on him by various of the close-knit cast of characters. The final effect of Amis's chosen point of view—though it sometimes teeters on the edge of uncertainty and seems to avoid authorial commitment—is to convey the genuine difficulty of moral judgments and, even more, the near-impossibility of helping people.

Douglas Yandell's situation is an unenviable one. Himself a good amateur pianist, would-be biographer of Weber and professional music critic, who contributes reviews of concerts to the right-wing newspaper edited by Harold Meers, Douglas is drawn into Roy's life as a result of having earlier on been "secretary to the orchestra of which Roy was then resident conductor." As a friend of Roy's, he is seen by Kitty Vandervane as someone who may be able to wean her husband away from a new affair that promises her the disaster, at nearly forty-seven, of being left. At the same time, Roy sees Douglas as a fellow male from whom he may charm various "favours": the loan of his flat for a night, the camouflage of his company when he takes out for the evening[6] a Sylvia growing more and more irritable at being hidden away. Throughout the novel, Douglas's sympathy for Kitty (and for Roy's drop-out daughter Penny, whom he both fancies and is sorry for) causes him to disapprove of Roy's unsuitable liaison and try to argue the case both for the dignity of "being one's age" and for orthodox domestic morality; yet a sort of reluctant admiration for Roy's ebullience, together with the respect of one professional musician for a better one, make him in effect as often Roy's "accomplice" as his "aunt" (Ch. 4).

Accused by Gilbert Alexander, in Chapter 1, of being an "imperialist racist fascist" on account of the newspaper he writes for, Douglas deflates the charge with a casual "I don't care about any of that, you see." Broadly speaking, this is true; though instinctively hostile to disorder, the spoiling of children, the bad, or nonexistent, manners of youth and their "uncouth minstrelsy" (Ch. 4), Douglas is politically neutral, able to praise a pianist without suppressing mention of his East German origin and to mock by hyperbole the right-wing bias of his editor: "a new Bolivian opera with a white Rhodesian conductor and a mixed cast of Brazilians, Haitians, Spaniards, white South Africans and members of the John Birch society" would be just the thing, he imagines, for Harold Meers. Even-handed, his ironic observation is brought to bear on the trendy left-wingery of Roy Vandervane, and in the hotch-potch of objects visible in Roy's house we first recognize the chasing after "uncritical" youth of an eminent musician who ought to know better. Roy's study, akin to Belinda's dressing table in *The Rape of the Lock*, contains busts of Beethoven and of Mao, photos of Brahms and Castro, posters of "Che Guevara, Ho Chi Minh, a nude couple making love and other key figures of the time," "copies of Hutchings on Mozart's piano concertos and Marcuse on liberation, posters announcing a Nikisch concert in 1913 and an anti-American demonstration in 1969."

In short, Roy Vandervane is a sort of Peter Pan, determined to renew his own youth and fit in with the present, and in his view Douglas is an "ole square." This very phrase belongs to a newly adopted form of pronunciation which, originating from Amis's disapproval (Roy "must have decided on the new slurring policy as more adaptable, better politically and like young people talked, too"), offers one of Amis's most diverting linguistic observations: "corm beef," "hambag," "tim peaches," "sweep pickle," "moce people," and (best of all) "foam book" and "scream play." The same thing may be said of Roy's "fuckettes," short phrases that have annoyed him and which he uses as exclamations of irritation: "school of thought," "sporting spirit," "Christian Gentleman" (Franco), "Peace in our time" (Chamberlain), "Puck-like theme," and (bringing in that American involvement in Vietnam which Amis himself unpopularly approved of) "Spiro Agnew." Perversely, while such phrases sharply indicate a fashionable radicalism which Douglas finds distasteful, their sheer proliferation conveys an irrepressible personality, bubbling with "rage at absent or largely imaginary foes," which it is hard to dislike.

More important than these linguistic externals, however, and more potentially harmful, are their corollaries in Roy's behavior: his devotion to Sylvia and his punningly entitled experimental composition "Elevations 9"—both of them, in Douglas's view, attempts to "arse-creep" youth. The former, if pursued, will betray Roy's marriage and jeopardize the future of his already-disturbed children; the latter, if performed as Roy intends with the caustically named pop group "Pigs Out," will betray not only Roy's considerable musical reputation but the cause of serious music itself. Although, at the end, Douglas conscientiously blames himself for the inadequacy of his "help" (Ch. 10), his feeling of guilt is unduly strong, for he expresses the case for marriage and music as forcefully as one feels any friend can; but it remains true that he fails, despite greasing Roy's bow before the "Pigs Out" concert in order to sabotage the performance and save Roy from making a fool of himself.

The splendidly sardonic Chapter 6 describes Roy's confrontation at the right-wing "Retrenchment Club" by Harold Meers. Meers is coldly determined, if Roy does not drop his daughter Sylvia, to expose his left-wing views and his cult of youth as a hypocritical sham, and the reader is led to feel that Roy, for once, is getting what his behavior deserves. The point is reinforced when he emerges from the club to find his car—in which he has placed "Support White Rhodesia" stickers to make people angry—with its tires slashed: his reflex of fury makes one realize that political anger and attacks on his property are not for him synonymous. In Chapter 9, however, which describes the night of the "Pigs Out" concert, one's feelings are all on Roy's side, and on Douglas's, who listens with a mixture of pleasure ("Elevations 9" is a flop) and intense embarrassed pity to the misplaced technical ingenuity which Roy brings to what turns out to be a far from "with-it" piece in remembered thirty-year-old jazz style:

Oh God, I thought, how could he not know that this lot positively disliked the idea of the difficult made to seem easy, seem anything at all, exist in any form—that what they liked was the easy seeming easy?

When, immediately afterwards, Roy is attacked by "yobbos," hits his head on the pavement, and has his Stradivarius smashed, one feels that he has plumbed the depths of humiliation and is likely to share Douglas's "feelings of anti-climax and defeat." What kind of a world, one wonders, has Roy got into?—particularly as the memory is still fresh of Sylvia's attempt to brain Kitty, who has tearfully tried to remonstrate with her (Ch. 5).

Yet, in the hospital, sad at the destruction of his violin and the failure of his piece, Roy is already bouncing back: he will continue his recording of all Mahler's symphonies, but he is also planning another "pop" composition. He has also decided, finally, to marry Sylvia, even though he is fully aware (Ch. 6) that she may not stay with him for more than a couple of years. But, though the novel gives no reason for this, he does not expect to live beyond sixty, and two years, at his age, is a long time. What Sylvia can give him, as has been indicated at a number of points earlier in the novel, is the spice of her availability and that of more exotic sex (like "going down"), an excitement akin to, but greater than, that felt by the "chap," mentioned in Chapter 2, "who said he couldn't read 'Girl, 20' in a small-ad column without getting the horn." When Kitty asks Sylvia in Chapter 5 what Roy sees in her, Sylvia calmly and cruelly strips to reveal a body which even Douglas, repelled by knowing it is Sylvia's, is forced to recognize as "a young body" and so, to that extent, unanswerable. Whether or not the feeling of Roy and Sylvia for each other is also "love" (as they both unemphatically claim), it is certainly, for a man who feels himself ageing, something stronger than responsibility, convention, and morality: "poor old sods at my time of life," Roy says in Chapter 1, "deserve [understanding] too, or anyway we need it, just starting to shape up to the idea of being dead or ole men." The decision to which this apparently light statement has led is greeted by Douglas with public, if unwilling, good wishes ("Well, goodbye. You bloody fool. And good luck. To both of you.") and by violent, private grief: "'Fuck,' I said. 'Shit. Oh God.'"[7]

The bleakness of this outcome—Douglas's failure to help Kitty and, as he sees it, to save Roy—is compounded by the succession of losses in the final chapter, which begins, by a stroke of ironic patterning, with a distorted echo of the opening phrase of Chapter 1, the word "bad" replacing the word "good." Douglas is sacked by Harold Meers; in part a vicarious act of revenge, which will have no great effect on Douglas's life. Then his girl, Vivienne, announces her engagement to Gilbert, whom she has met earlier on the doorstep of Douglas's flat. Douglas, liberal and lukewarm, has not objected either to her being "shared" with another man or to her overfancy clothes, since his inclination is to let adults do what they want; he is also less involved that way. Gilbert, more decisive, less chary of responsibility, objects to both clothes and sharing: an attitude which (rather unfairly and late in the day, one

feels) she finds preferable.[8] Douglas can let her go without rancor, and
his attitudes are hardly reprehensible; but his meeting with Mr. Copes
in Chapter 7, in its exposure of his lack of interest in religion or "something more than just this world," seems intended to suggest something
Laodicean about him. As Mr. Copes gently says:

Very, very nearly everybody who's ever done anything has believed in something, and by anything I don't mean anything important, I mean anything
whatever.[9]

The implication that something is missing in Douglas—that, perhaps, his devotion to music is not enough—hardly explains his failure
to change the fates of the elder Vandervanes, nor does it do justice to
his strongly felt offer (expressed in Chapter 3) to "take on" Penny Vandervane, who repudiates it. But the sense of some shortcoming remains
in the reader's mind, and in Douglas's, as he confronts the two last
shocks the novel has to offer: the results, felt indirectly by the "Furry
Barrel" and directly by Penny, of Roy's defection from his family
responsibilities. Arriving at the Vandervane's house, hoping that at last
he will be able to rescue Penny (about whom he does care, and whom
he is willing to make, in Vivienne's phrase, his "number one priority"),
he finds the dog limping on three legs, having been permanently crip-
pled by "a kicking" from Ashley, the six-year-old, ghastly child whom
Roy has "spoiled rotten" and who has now left with his deserted
mother, for whom "Roy and Roy's world" were everything. The
moment is small, but infinitely moving:

I stooped down and stroked the dog's silky head, feeling as if something dismal had happened right in the middle of my own life and concerns, something major, something irretrievable, as if I had taken a fatally wrong decision years before and only now seen how much I had lost by it.

Penny, whom the family tension was previously "destroying" (Ch. 4),
seems strangely better, straightfowardly friendly, interested again in
classical music. In fact, she has given up struggling against a life in
which "there's nothing I'd like to do" (Ch. 3): her present serenity—
touching, beautiful, horrible—is due to heroin, and her short life-
expectation (two years, like the lease on Sylvia her father anticipates)
is precisely what she welcomes: "Nothing's going to last." The ironic
gaiety of her final words—"We're all free now," a statement all the

more devastating for being sincerely meant, as if, indeed, no one is to blame—expands the novel's acid commentary on the "permissive society" into a blank, staring desolation—a grim parody of existential openness—which is without parallel in Amis's fiction.

II   Ending Up *(1974)*

The material of *Ending Up*, Amis's shortest but not short-seeming novel, "incubated for about three years," and was suggested by the "species of commune" at his own house, Lemmons, "with relations and people living in."[10] "What," Amis wondered, "would this sort of arrangement be like if one had a pack of characters who were all about 20 years older?"

Pretty grim, one concludes from the result, whose claustrophobic sense of the limitations of old age is prefigured by instances in three earlier novels by Amis. First there is Patrick Standish's depressing encounter with the ageing Lord Edgerstoune, who has discovered that, though you think you can still do things, you find in practice that you can't (*Take a Girl like You*, Ch. 20). There is the narrow range of activities available to Maurice Allington's "ancient and decrepit" father, seventy-nine and with three strokes behind him, who dies of a cerebral hemorrhage caused by fright. The loneliness of old age and the horror of death are reflected in Maurice's pitying comment: "We don't know what he suffered" (*The Green Man*, Part I). Finally, in *Girl, 20*, Douglas and Kitty, on their way to the local pub, pass "an old people's home from which old people stared resentfully out at us" (Ch. 5). There is little enough in the lot of these two worth envying; but at least they are outside, and can move about.

All these elements—incapacity, loneliness, restriction, resentment—are experienced in various forms, and to a varying extent, by the five old people, aged between seventy and seventy-five, who have "ended up" in an isolated, chilly cottage seven miles from Newmarket. Its name, Tuppenny-hapenny Cottage,[11] is embarrassingly quaint, but also suggests the economies to which middle-class people of its denizens' generation have been reduced after retirement: plastic-looking ham, margarine to eke out the butter, South African sherry, Tunisian red wine, British vermouth. Such details of necessitous expediency provide the novel with a faint, dismal undertone throughout, as does the silting-up in the cottage of a jarring medley of prized possessions of little relevance to the realities of their owners' present lives. The past may have led to and conditioned the present, but it is now "a foreign country: they do things differently there."[12] The wider present is also remote: Bernard Bastable reflects of his newspaper (the *Daily Telegraph*) that "it and its contemporaries seemed like parish magazines of another parish than his own" (Ch. 6). And the two visits by Marigold Pyke's reluctant, dutiful, kind grandchildren and their families, welcome to all but Bernard, only demonstrate the vast generation gap between young people active in such unfamiliar occupations as "electrics, or electronics" (Ch. 28) and advertising, and old people born before the Great War (Adela even smells old) who have nothing to do but endure their afflictions, tick off the days and even the hours, and occupy themselves in activities that as often irritate as assist each other. It may be a sign of excessive pessimism in Amis that all his characters are made to face the pains and futilities of old age as early as in their seventies, but given such a group's assembly in a confined space, what follows in the novel is not hard to believe; especially as Amis's subject is not just old age and decay, but the exacerbation (and sometimes the amelioration) of those inevitabilities by the interaction of different human temperaments. Old people are old; but they are also people.

The novel, which begins in October 1972, covers what turn out to be the last three months in the lives of all five. Only two, Adela Bastable and her brother Bernard (the oldest, at seventy-five), go further than the confines of the cottage and its adjacent woods, Adela twice to Newmarket to do the shopping, Bernard once to London to see a specialist. The only visitors, apart from the doctor, come primarily to see Marigold (Adela's friend since schooldays in 1912): her grandchildren Trevor and Rachel, their spouses and children. Neither the visits to places (which are not described) nor the visits from relatives bring the reader much sense of relief, in terms of reassurance that a larger world exists beyond the cottage and its inhabitants, the other two of whom are Derrick Shortell ("Shorty"), Bernard's former soldier-servant and onetime lover, and George Zeyer, Bernard's brother-in-law as the result of a shortlived marriage now over thirty years in the past. The novel thus has no striking plot, and nothing "important" happens.

Instead, in a sequence of forty short chapters, Amis magnifies the minutiae of daily behavior, employing a third-person narration which accommodates a few direct authorial comments but mainly moves, with unobtrusive skill, to and fro between the externals of action and the inner worlds of the characters' minds. While authorial description permits much comedy, the character's thoughts and feelings provoke sympathy and sometimes, as particularly with Adela and George, admiration. Behind the battery of illness—Adela's gastric ulcer, Bernard's piles and his convenient but real gammy leg, Shorty's drunkenness, enlarged liver and chronic diarrhea, George's semiparalysis and nominal aphasia, Marigold's worsening amnesia—real human beings, devoted, malicious, obliging, hopeful, affected, will not lie down. The slow-motion quality of Amis's presentation (fourteen chapters for the first day, nine for Christmas Day) conveys both the slowness and boredom of their lives and, for most of them, the importance of what little they still have. In formal terms, the many small chapters, apportioned laterally between groupings of characters as well as inching forward in time, resemble the progress of a ballet or an opera: solo arias, duets, trios, choruses, as the characters separate and rejoin on their various short-range errands. A further, external perspective is provided by the relatives' visits (Bernard's "real anger and hatred" are disquietingly evident to Trevor Fishwick at the end of Chapter 10); by the realization that a horrible and pathetic old age is what most of us must face, which comes to Trevor and to Keith MacKelvie in Chapter 29; and by the sad and gruesome final chapter, in which Bernard is seen by his long-forgotten son Stanley as "a trousered human leg" poking out of a leaf-strewn heap of sacking, then as an only dimly remembered face: the constant movement between man as subject and man as object which Amis's technique allows is frozen finally by death into the latter category.

Bernard, Adela, and Shorty have been at the cottage since 1961; Marigold, widowed[13] and with a stage career "undistinguished and brief" far behind her, since 1969; George for only five months, after a stroke has paralyzed his right side. Out of the friction between them, cooped up in a small house with a cat and an ancient bull-terrier to complicate matters, comes a great deal of comic incident, ornamented by idiosyncrasies of language and shot through with petty malice. It is the two newest arrivals who, through no real fault of their own, give rise to the sharpest irritation, partly because they own the two animals (which brings them into defensive rivalry with each other), partly because of the way they talk. George Zeyer, a former professor,[14] combines inability to remember nouns with reluctance to stop talking: "Did you watch, you know, the thing on the switching it on last night?" (Ch. 4). Bernard's careful, lying negative only releases a flood of similar halting periphrases used to describe something on the radio. Marigold, the well-preserved remains of a "Bright Young Thing," annoys Bernard, and embarrasses others, by her theatrical affectations and her habit, originally an attention-seeking device, of speaking in excruciating diminutives: "drinkle-pinkle," "bootle-pootles," "blackle-packles," "tunkalunks" (for "thanks"). Shorty, whose residence in the house involves doing many of the chores, resents Marigold's attitude of superiority to "lower-class persons who had come the smallest distance up in the world" (Ch. 7), and would dearly love to thrust a "red-hot pokie-wokie" up Marigold's usually sedentary "arsle-parcel." All he does, however, is spill some Benedictine over her dress on Christmas Day, to which she responds by pushing him nearly into the fire (Ch. 34).

For Shorty is generally good-natured, with a flow of old-soldier humor and idiomatic mimicry ("grassy-arse, seen yours"), which recalls Harry Bannion in *I Like It Here*. He agrees "with animation" to Trevor's suggestion (Ch. 7) that the bedridden George be carried downstairs to lunch, and it is he himself who suggests a sing-song with carols at Christmas. His wants are simple: his "squaddie's literal seventh heaven" (Ch. 13) consists of being "dry, warm, indoors, off duty, smoking, pissed, and getting more pissed still." Despite his excessive drinking, and his casual attitude to cleaning the kitchen floor, he is one of the two pillars on whom the house depends. The other is Adela, whose largely unsuccessful search for love in her lonely earlier life makes her positively, if pathetically, happy in her present one, in which "there was always a job to do, and there always would be, with luck" (Ch. 26). Physically ugly, slow on the uptake, and with a voice which unfortunately conveys a "mild resentment" she rarely feels, and a domineering nature she does not possess, Adela is the closest the novel comes to an example of Christian forebearance and goodwill, and also of humility. There is sharp irony in the "acute self-reproach" she feels at not having herself thought that George could be brought downstairs: "She must make a real effort to think of others for a change" (Ch. 10). George, like Marigold, is fully aware of her virtues, telling her that "none of the rest of us would probably be alive if it weren't for you" (Ch. 11).

George himself, his hope and interest in life revived by the small change of coming downstairs, is both a pathetic and an admirable character. His physical affliction is obviously the greatest, but he is determined to be no more of a nuisance than he must be, to devise more efficient periphrases to counter his nounlessness, and to make some attempt (by sending to a learned journal an unfashionable defense of General Mihailović[15]) to resume his academic endeavors. And if Marigold's "grande dame" affectations irritate, there is also a touching dignity in her attempts to conceal what she thinks of as "senility": her increasing inability to remember things (like writing and receiving letters) which culminates in her total loss of the past, her happily married life (Ch. 31). It is this that decides her, finally, not to go into an old people's home: at the cottage there are people who themselves remember some of her past, through whom she may still feel vicariously connected to it.

The external view of old age's grotesqueries and afflictions, and the internal view of its partial pathos, which *Ending Up* undoubtedly presents, may well leave the reader sharing the pity and fear of Trevor Fishwick on Christmas Day:

They can't help it (he gabbled silently) they've got nothing to look foward to it's just got to be accepted you'll be like it yourself one day you'll be out of here soon oh Christ. (Ch. 31)

But against this, and against Keith MacKelvie's query whether old people think about death all the time (Ch. 29),[16] one needs to set the state of mind of George, Marigold, and Adela on New Year's Eve: "Each was, if not exactly happy, at any rate content" (Ch. 38). It is a brave contentment, quite without illusions, which Shorty, if he were awake, would probably share.

Bernard Bastable (bastard?), it is certain, would not. Bernard does think about death, and finds old age hard to bear, well before he discovers (in Chapter 18, but the reader is not allowed the knowledge until Chapter 37, and the other characters never know) that he has what appears to be bowel cancer, and only about three months to live. The effect of the withholding of this knowledge (though hints are dropped by references to the specialist Brownjohn[17]) is that the reader continues to find Bernard's characteristically outrageous behavior both extremely funny and utterly reprehensible. In his malice and resentment he is the dynamic principle of the novel, even though Amis refuses to allow his nastiest actions to come off: "Operation Stink," aimed against Marigold, fails to work (Ch. 27); "Operation Incontinence," aimed against Shorty, who has defended George against his more than usually outspoken rudeness, fails to worry its unwitting victim (Ch. 32). Bernard's resentment is as wide-ranging as Roger Mich-

eldene's, directed equally at Trevor for having too much hair on his
face and at Keith for having none. His malice finds targets in Adela for
her verbal obtuseness, in Marigold for her airs and graces, and in
George for his garrulity, particularly when he gains his best Christmas
present of all, a plethora of remembered nouns which Bernard does
not delight in. What Bernard thinks of George and Marigold, and what
Marigold thinks of Bernard, is cleverly indicated by the definitions
they offer, during the Christmas game of "Call My Bluff,"[18] of the
words "nemel," "jimp," and "spronk" (Ch. 34). Though Bernard
retains a vestige of "the habit of wanting to be mistaken for a man of
ordinary decent feeling" (Ch. 9), it cannot overcome a five-year-old
realization that "he had become incapable of either respect or affection" for others (Ch. 14).

While for Bernard, in Sartre's phrase, "Hell is other people," hell is
also himself, and it is this fact, as well as old age and the approach of
death, which such activities as water-pistol attacks on Pusscat, and plots
to discredit George's dog Mr. Pastry—distorted, shrunken reenact-
ments of an ex-brigadier's military operations— are designed to dis-
tract him from, so that he finally appears as a pitiful figure, while not
ceasing to be an unpleasant one. For him, despite a ten-day period
after his fatal news in which he tries to behave better, nobility does not
come with suffering, nor does he attain a serene appreciation of things
outside himself, like landscape, or some total picture of his life which
"might have been some compensation for having had to be Bernard
Bastable, for having had to live" (Ch. 37). It is as if one were listening
to Maurice Allington—or rather, to a Maurice Allington unvisited by
God—twenty years on. For Bernard, life is a burden, which weighs
more if you have a nasty temperament.

Bernard's death at the end (Ch. 39), falling off the ladder he has
laboriously climbed to cut the telephone wires, and so deprive Marigold of a call she is looking forward to, is an accident he deserves; but
it is also a laying down of his burden and a final, meaningless gesture
of nihilistic assertion, a last military operation. The other four deaths
which accompany Bernard's do not stem from his action; rather they
are a species of authorial mercy-killing, to which one might apply
Shorty's phrase "Heap big chief coming to put paid to palaver." Their
crescendo of black farce reduces what would otherwise be, if the
deaths were dragged out, unbearably saddening: we accept them,
bearing in mind Hamlet's phrase "If it be not now, yet it will come,"
and better, perhaps, for such an interdependent group to go together.

Yet, taken individually, all the deaths are characteristic of those who die, and convey pathos and a real sense of waste. Shorty dies of a drunken, partly semantic mistake, confusing white coagulant with colorless aperient; Marigold of forgetfulness and mild malice combined, tripping on Mr. Pastry's ball which she herself has deliberately left on the stairs; George (with an implied and horrible lack of immediacy) as a result of hearing Marigold's cry and trying to help—one might say he dies of decent feeling; Adela dies of the pressure of caring, the shock of a heart attack (hinted at in Chapter 10) on discovering the body of her only close friend, Marigold. And even Bernard's death, the result of a hostility he already knows is hollow, is given pathos when he is discovered by Stanley, on an accidental visit which yet hints at the different sort of life Bernard might have had. Much of *Ending Up* is a sustained exercise in mercilessly cutting observation, both of old age itself and of the antics with which it is confronted, and one cannot deny its power to amuse: Bernard is not the only one whom malicious jokes make to laugh till he cries (Ch. 25). But the restraint Amis achieves in his actual narrative style, and the comprehensive understanding he brings to the novel's representative range of characters, make *Ending Up* also a frightening *memento mori* and a notable extension of his compassion.

III   Jake's Thing (1978)

After the various kinds of authorial self-restraint demonstrated by *The Riverside Villas Murder, Ending Up,* and *The Alteration,* Amis's most recent novel, *Jake's Thing,* gives the impression of a release of control, a relaxation into resentful realism, welcome no doubt to its author but resulting in a book which is too confused and sprawling to make a really powerful impact. Amis himself, in an interview published in 1974, clearly sees nothing wrong in the novel's being—in Henry James's phrase—a "loose baggy monster":

. . . the novel being such an elastic form, a ragbag in which you can put anything, and novelists being human, the novel is a platform from which they can deal out digs and unpleasant remarks and little bits of satire lasting a paragraph or two at a time, because there's room for that.[19]

The trouble with *Jake's Thing* (as with *Take a Girl like You,* the predecessor it in this way resembles[20]) is partly that the paragraphs of tangential satire are often too long, partly that they are often devoted to matters hardly worth the bother: the imagined television "script conference" (Ch. 3), the cover summary of *The Hippogriff Attaché-Case* (Ch. 10), the description of the Chinese wine Wan Fu (Ch. 14), the matter of Stanton St. Leonard churchyard (Ch. 20), the three passages which the protagonist reads between visual stimulations at the sex laboratory in Colliers Wood (Ch. 8)—passages not apparently chosen for any light, ironic or otherwise, which they might cast on the story. Nevertheless, for all its self-indulgent proliferation, the novel also contains a good deal of gloomily pointed writing: much can be forgiven a book which includes what is surely one of Amis's most brilliantly sardonic one-liners, describing the beverage available at the encounter group weekend held somewhere near Salisbury: "You got your coffee out of a machine, and having done that you couldn't get it back in" (Ch. 25).

The witty despair of this remark typifies the unloveliness of the contemporary England in which the protagonist finds himself: a world of soaring costs ("he laid out his fifty quid or whatever it was for a second-class ticket"), encroachment by non-Caucasians, the crumbling remains of academic comfort, and the increasingly brazen trumpet notes of the "monstrous regiment of women," who constitute for the protagonist both his public and his private problem. His arrival in Oxford for the summer term of 1977 is summed up in a phrase that deliberately recalls, and cancels, the preference of Garnet Bowen twenty years before: "Jake knew where he was at once without liking it there" (Ch. 10).

Even more explicitly, however, and more comprehensively, the disenchantment of *Jake's Thing* is offered as a contrast to the hopefulness of Amis's first novel, *Lucky Jim*. *Jake's Thing* is his only other novel to have a university teacher for its protagonist (one who has stayed the course, produced four books, and attained the prestigious rank of Reader[21]) and to be set, at least for nine of its twenty-eight chapters,[22] in an academic environment, in this case a fictitious college in the University of Oxford; and where Jim taught Medieval History, Jake teaches Early Mediterranean History. The protagonists' names are disguised reflections of each other: Jake (Jaques) - Jacques - James (Jim); Richardson - Dick's son - Dixon; and in the "attempted suicide" of Kelly,[23] which Jake is summoned, unknowingly, to witness or interrupt (Chs. 24–25), there is an obvious recollection of the suicide attempt of Margaret Peel, though here, more darkly, Jake is not allowed to shrug off a feeling of personal responsibility that is at least equally uncalled for. That these similarities go deeper than externals is strongly indicated by a passage in Chapter 3, in which Jake looks out of the window of his house in the imaginary suburb of "Orris Park" (superimposed on the Ken Wood section of Hampstead), and thinks of his early days there:

Then as now there had been plenty to see, mainly by the street-lamp that stood no more than twenty yards off: houses, trees, bushes, parked cars, the bird-table in the garden diagonally opposite. Then, too, some of the windows must have been illuminated and it was quite possible that, as now, the only sounds had been faint voices and distant footsteps. After some effort he remembered further his feelings of curiosity, almost of expectation, as if he might find himself seeing a link between that moment and things that had happened earlier in his life.

What Jake's memory is unsuccessfully reaching back to discover is, one suspects, that happiness to which Jim Dixon looks forward, as he glimpses in "the badly-lit jakes" (*Lucky Jim*, Ch. 2) a vision of some as yet unvisited part of London.

Jake Richardson has kept his academic career, and still—with his one interested and congenial pupil Mr. Thwaites—derives some small pleasure from it; though he has no intention of writing any more books, he does eventually finish an article on ancient Syracuse which in the final chapter he sends off to a learned journal. But he has not kept his first wife and is now, at fifty-nine, on his third, Brenda, who is approaching forty-eight. Or rather, he is not on her, since he has lost his libido and is sexually unresponsive not only to his "fat wife" but "even girls I can see are very attractive" (Ch. 4). This problem gives point to his full name, Jaques: clearly meant to recall the saturnine commentator of *As You Like It*, it puts the reader in mind of the very last stage of his "Seven Ages of Man" speech, "Sans teeth, sans eyes, sans taste, sans every thing" (*AYLI*, II, vii, 166). Jake's "thing" (all, as yet, that he is without) is his penis, for whose improvement his psychiatrist, a small Irishman reductively named Proinsias Rosenberg, recommends a course of "inceptive regrouping" preceded by masturbation to "pictorial pornographic material," the writing out of sexual fantasies, "non-genital" (and later genital) "sensate focussing sessions" with Brenda, and the embarrassing attentions of a gadget called the "nocturnal mensurator."

To some degree the cogency of Jake's physical problem, which for
much of the novel he tries with mingled conscientiousness and distaste
to overcome, depends on how far the reader feels that, for a man of
nearly sixty, it really matters. The reader would not, perhaps, even in
relation to the older people of whom she is thinking, let alone in relation to someone a decade or so younger, wholly assent to Tracy Fishwick's proposition in *Ending Up:* "the idea of sex in any relation to
the old, any relation at all, was obscene" (Ch. 7). Yet he may wonder,
nevertheless, whether the awkwardnesses, and contortions, of fondling
by numbers, the probings of sex questionnaires, and the indignities of
encounter groups like that "At Mr. Shyster's" (Chs. 15–16) represent
a higher price than any older man, especially an alleged Oxford don,
would pay for the possible restoration of virility. Any doubts about the
importance, at such an age, of sex per se would, however, gain much
of their force from the implicit assumption that, after all, other things
would make up for its decline: companionship, mutual interests, shared
memories, the common denominator in all these being an underlying
liking and respect for one's marriage partner—in effect, an interest in
women as people.

It is precisely the lack in Jake of this interest that gradually reveals
itself, to him and to the reader, as his real problem, his real "thing,"
and while the novel explores, and even exploits, for satirical and also
nostalgic ends, the byways of his sexual therapy, what emerges is their
essential pointlessness. From being, in the comically pronounced words
of Ernie, the college porter who is Amis's prime verbal creation in the
novel, a "ruddy uncraned king" of sex (Ch. 10), Jake has become a
man whose attitude to women is akin to his attitude to gardening: he
can't "be fucking bothered" (Ch. 26). Since his wife is forty-eight, and
still interested in sex, Jake perseveres out of compunction and is able
to make love to her on a single occasion; but in his dealings with Kelly,
the twenty-year-old disturbed girl who fancies him, he is—at least sexually—a "mace" rather than a man, calling on her "in a frightened
voice to leave him alone" (Ch. 21). On the one occasion in the novel
when he makes love willingly, to one of his old flames, Eve Greenstreet,
the act is significantly not described, and it transpires (Ch. 19) that he
did so (and also got drunk) because he could not stand her verbal mannerisms any longer. (This is not surprising in view of Eve's gangster-
imitation style of talk, but her manner—"like Mencken but sexy with
it"—is hard to credit, and one suspects Amis of rigging the evidence
here.)

Thus, though the statistics of his earlier track-record—Jake tells Dr. Rosenberg that "in my time I've been to bed with well over a hundred women" (Ch. 4)—together with the nervous residue of affection for his wife, furnish a plausible surface reason for his tolerance of psychiatric practices clearly repellent to him, the very fact of his having slept with so many women argues the lack of interest in them as people, indeed the hostility to most of them, that is his final recognition not only about his present self but about his past one. Both his wife, who tells Rosenberg that Jake sees women only as "sexual pabulum" (Ch. 12), and Eve Greenstreet, whose current experience of Jake contradicts her memories of him and causes her, now, to agree with Brenda, only anticipate what Jake himself ruefully admits to his homosexual Oxford colleague Damon Lancewood: "I don't even like them much. Women. I despise them intellectually. [. . .] I'm a male chauvinist pig" (Ch. 22). Eventually, though he is sorry to see Brenda leave him for the dim, colorless Geoffrey Mabbott, he cannot summon the energy of valid protest, unable now to remember with any of its original intense happiness even their holiday six years before at an archaeological site in Turkey: "To look back on it now was a bit like looking at a museum postcard of some archaic wall-painting or mosaic" (Ch. 26).

As well as suggesting the two kinds of "thing" about Jake, physical and mental, which the novel investigates, its title inevitably calls up the notion of "doing one's own thing." What this means, for Jake, is made clear right at the end when Dr. Curnow mentions the lately discovered possibility that his libido may be restored simply "by taking something." Reeling off in his head a long, fluent diatribe on the shortcomings and nuisance-value of women, Jake finds it easy to refuse the opportunity: for him, as for Jim Dixon, but to very different effect, experience brings the knowledge of what one is, and the pressure to act accordingly. What the innocent Hubert Anvil does his best to retain, Jake willingly surrenders. Whereas, for Brenda, the sex drive constitutes "ballast" in human relationships and enables people to see clearly, for Jake it has been a set of blinkers concealing the intrinsic boringness of the women who were its objects; or perhaps simply, as he puts it to Lancewood (Ch. 22), "it was just that in those days I was a normal man with a normal interest in women and now I'm not."

Whether one finally agrees with Brenda or with Jake, whether one feels Jake's decision to be a clear-eyed refusal of blinkers or a lightheaded refusal of ballast, depends to some extent on factors external to the novel: on the importance one attaches to continued sexual activity, or to the less physical aspects of relationships with women; on the accidents of one's own experience; on the accident of what gender one happens to be. Though it involves the setting aside, in effect, of half the human race, and carries with it a proportionate degree of loneliness, Jake's decision is offered by Amis with an appearance of lightness, and also with a qualification ostensibly intended to exclude the author: Jake's diatribe is parenthetically described as "all according to him." Amis has stated that "I don't have these problems"[24] and that the novel originated not from direct experience but from "the reading of two sexual therapy books," conversation with "a woman informant," and a meal at All Souls' College, Oxford, at which he learned that the "big issue there . . . was the admission of women to men's colleges [. . .] it all clicked."[25] Nevertheless, though Amis uses third-person narrative, and for the sake of fairness allows Jake to be struck once, unwillingly, by the shrewdness and competence of the encounter group's American "facilitator" Ed (Ch. 15), and Brenda to assert that some members of the group are genuinely helped by his methods (Ch. 26), such force as *Jake's Thing* possesses is felt most strongly when Jakes's own consciousness (the observing medium of the novel) is brought to bear in all its "contempt, hatred, weariness and malicious hilarity" (Ch. 22) on uncongenial phenomena; and what it feels frequently squares with recent statements made by Amis himself, in poetry and in polemical prose.

That consciousness, as hostile as Jim Dixon's to the "pseudo-light" shed on "non-problems," not this time by learned articles but by the methods, "intellectually beneath contempt," of modern psychiatry, is decidedly prejudiced, but it is not unimpressive. Whether Jake really suffers, as Rosenberg claims, from "guilt and shame" in his attitudes to sex seems doubtful; what is clear is that, basically, he considers private matters to be private (Ch. 25) and is not at home in a world where the female genitals, to him as exotic, and irrelevant, as "the inside of a giraffe's ear or a tropical fruit not much prized even by the locals" (Ch. 5), are exposed in isolation in magazines like *Mezzanine* and *Kensington*.[26] His own upbringing has been on the less explicit magazines of three decades ago,[27] and the innocence, and nostalgia, of his tastes are made clear at the sex laboratory, where he chooses out of more crudely stimulating photographs one of a girl "who, by the look of her, could have no idea in the world why those men had asked her to lean against a tree wearing just a straw hat" (Ch. 8). Such romantically sexual tastes, touchingly old-fashioned, are equally unsatisfied by the lumpishly dressed modern girl-in-the street, about whom Amis has spoken with-eringly, if more briefly, in his poem "Shitty":[28]

> They were wearing curtains, blankets, table-cloths, loose covers off armchairs and sofas. A sideboard-runner hung around one neck in the manner of a stole, a doubled-over loop of carpet round another in that of an academic hood. And somebody's fucking them, thought Jake. (Ch. 5)

Jake's description is impressionistically fair, his incredulity sympa-thetic: well, in such a world, may the libido of a man of his generation wither, and even more when suffering from "a couple of smart tweaks of the hampton" inflicted by girls demonstrating against the "élite chauvinism" of Jake's all-male college (Ch. 10).

The "indefensibly ludicrous proposition" that he is about to be sixty is greeted by Jake very much in the manner of the early, ironical Gar-net Bowen:

> Well, at least no one could say he was wiser or more sensible or understood anything better along with it. (Ch. 26)

There are times when the reader may easily agree, as with his farci-cally hostile attempt (Ch. 2) to deprive Alcestis Mabbott of the good claret he has bought at "Winesteals, Ltd."; his lack of success, as like Graham Greene's "whisky priest" in *The Power and the Glory* he watches her drink it, may well prompt the reaction Jake has himself when Ed hits the aggressive Chris at the encounter group: "He felt a sudden sharp twinge of total lack of pity for him" (Ch. 15). Yet behind Jake's prejudices there are attitudes with which one can sympathize, attitudes which are no worse than out of place in the world he has survived into. That the object of Jake's academic hostility in Chapter 11 should be a female, rather than a male, student is not very plausible, given the acute competition for women's places at Oxford Colleges, nor does the esoteric nature of Miss Calvert's chosen special subject, Minoan, suggest the lack of academic motivation indicated by Amis; but the faults Jake seethes over—poor spelling, illegibility, complacent ignorance—are themselves all too frequent in students of both sexes. And whether or not one is convinced by the sexist "reasoning" behind Jake's resistance to the admission of women to "Comyns College," there is no mistaking the depth of his feelings, as at the college meet-ing, inspired by "rage and dizziness," he passes from the "pro" case he has been asked to make (and makes quite well, if halfheartedly) to the "con" case in which he really believes:

. . . there will be women everywhere, chattering, gossiping, telling you what they did today and what their daughter did yesterday and what their friend did last week and what somebody they heard about did last month and horrified if a chap brings up a *topic* or an *argument*. They don't mean what they say, they don't use language for discourse but for extending their personality, they take all disagreement as opposition, yes they do, even the brightest of them, and that's the end of the search for truth which is what the whole thing's supposed to be about. (Ch. 20)

Jake *is* his age, even if he neither feels it nor always acts it, and though, unlike Maurice Allington, he does not fear death, the hollow sort of life, "troubled with excessive shitting," which he is left with at the end of the novel is neither to be envied nor chuckled over: a shuttling between "a perfectly bearable couple of rooms in Kentish Town" with no wife (thankfully) to make every square foot "nice," and an Oxford less and less likely to provide the "sense of safety" he finds in Damon Lancewood's rooms (Ch. 22). As he journeys, bearing an unspecified guilt for his failure to help Kelly—a daughter-figure, perhaps—one may imagine the recurrence in him of what he feels in Chapter 10 as the train stops for a moment beside an Oxford cemetery:

The thought of shortly arriving in some such place himself and staying there meant little to Jake [. . .] but this afternoon there was that in what he saw which dispirited him. In the circumstances he was quite grateful for the yards of rusty galvanised iron fences, piles of rubble and of wrecked cars and, further off, square modern buildings which helped to take his mind off such matters.[29]

CHAPTER 8

"A Higher Art": Amis's Poetry

K INGSLEY Amis was a poet before he was a novelist. He wrote poetry while at the City of London School, and six of the poems in his first collection date from before the autumn of 1943. He has published six separate volumes of poems, together with a *Collected Poems* subsuming most of their contents and adding some twenty more poems, between 1947 and 1979; so that his poetry spans his entire writing career and often, though also being of considerable interest for its own sake, sheds directly personal light on attitudes in his novels which are mediated through created characters.

Amis has stated that "I'm delighted when I can write a poem."[1] He has not been prolific, having produced only about 130 poems in over thirty-five years; his rate over the past decade has been no more than two poems a year. But considering that his friend and contemporary Philip Larkin has published rather fewer poems over the same period, Amis's total—for a writer so active in other fields—is a very respectable one, and his level of technical accomplishment is consistently medium to high, at least after 1947. Nevertheless, it would do Amis no service to overestimate his achievement as a poet; he has spoken of poetry itself as being "a higher art"[2] than fiction, but his own lasting reputation is likely to be based mainly on his novels. When his *Collected Poems* appeared in 1979, Amis was praised by Anthony Powell as "one of our very best poets," a verdict endorsed fulsomely by Clive James, and implicitly by Philip Toynbee, who pronounced "perhaps 50" of the poems included to be "very good."[3] The sincerity of these views may well have included an admixture of respect for a writer established as important by other means, who had also written good poems; and that respect may have been extended as much to "persistence and perseverance"—authorial qualities Amis himself values[4]— as to accomplishment.

I should not, myself, make such large claims for Amis's poetry: some of it is no more than sharp, well-turned verse, and little of it possesses

the emotional and intellectual resonance to be found in the work of
contemporaries such as Donald Davie, Keith Douglas (killed in 1944),
and, most of all, Philip Larkin. Even though, in his poetry, he often
speaks with a memorable crispness and individuality, Amis only rarely
uncovers that deepest level in himself which would cause the reader's
imagination and heart to vibrate in sympathy, rarely obeys the injunction stated at the end of one of his most eloquent and justly anthologized poems of the 1950s, "Masters":

> By yielding mastery the will is freed,
> For it is by surrender that we live,
> And we are taken if we wish to give,
> Are needed if we need.[5]

I   Bright November (1947)

When, as a young poet, Amis was more inclined to emotional self-
revelation, he lacked both a personal voice and the technical assurance
which might have allowed him to be simultaneously emotional and
cogent. For many years the Penguin issues of his novels were accompanied by his declaration that "until 24, I was in all departments of
writing *abnormally unpromising*,"[6] and since few of the poems which
appeared in his first volume, *Bright November*, can have been written
after 1946, one must assume that Amis's statement is meant to include
them. His omission of the volume from his *Who's Who* entry argues
a negative attitude toward it, an attitude reinforced by his relieved
reaction when Clive James suggested to him that, as a collector's item,
it must now be "worth a bomb": "Good. That'll keep its circulation
nicely restricted."[7] Of its thirty-one poems, he has chosen to reprint
only six in his *Collected Poems*, two of which, "Bed and Breakfast"
and "Beowulf," also found their way, substantially altered, into his
fourth volume, *A Case of Samples* (1956). The alterations, in part,
reveal changing influences rather than self-discovery. W. H. Auden is
perhaps the strongest influence (e.g., in a phrase like "the jutting knees
of the preoccupied"[8]) on Amis's poetry in the 1940s, Robert Graves in
the 1950s; both of them inescapable influences for many young poets
in those two periods.

Amis has spoken of Auden's poetry as helping him, but also as hindering "by suggesting that riddles were okay."[9] Throughout *Bright
November*, certainly, one has the recurrent sense of subject matter

never quite brought into focus, either blurred into a vaguely gesturing portentousness:

> I speak the word Man, random meeting of events,
> Bereaved of articulation, dear temporary one;
> The reaction of acids beyond his own secretion,
> Unexciting reflection of objects not his own. . . .
> (Poem XIII)

or thrown away in a kind of nervous understatement, as at the end of "Radar," which appears to contrast the innocence of scientific discovery and what happens afterwards, the invention of the cathode-ray tube and its development into the airborne radar of World War II:

> On the enemy side stood aerials like the bereaved
> Who mask their essence with respectable sound;
> And Kolster and Dunmore heard their interference,
> But it was dismissed by them as a stray effect.

Both these poems are described in Amis's prefatory note to *Bright November* as "early work," produced before October 1943, but later poems in the volume are no less characteristically "fortyish," combining the scientific vocabulary of Auden with romantic feeling, an obscure personal distress. "Elisabeth's Intermezzo" contains the line "Our closeness was an exponential term" and "For Elisabeth's Birthday," which begins with a sequence of five definite article phrases in the manner of Auden, ends thus:

> So on your birthday I make these diagnoses
> Dried with the heat of anger, and my wish
> Is for the renewal of the charges of love
> In the hidden metal wickedly vitiated.

Bright November is Amis's only volume to contain love poems directed to a named person (there are few love poems of any sort in his later ones); its dedication is "For Elisabeth," and five poems mention her in their titles. Of these Amis has preserved in *Collected Poems* "Letter to Elisabeth," whose iambic couplets, employing half-rhyme throughout, suggest either the influence of Wilfred Owen direct, or of Owen filtered through Auden, the first important poet to copy his technique. Despite the poem's claim that "love has taught me to speak

straight," the situation it expresses is unclear, but its mingled feelings
of regret and hope are conveyed with some youthful force:

> A time for feeling,
> Uniting lovers in the spring, fulfilling
> The fumbling gesture and the hoarded pain,
> The static hand of love wrenching the pen,
> Shall come to us in our new year, shall come
> As certainly as separation came. . . .

More nakedly powerful, in its very vulnerability, is another love poem,
"Where Are You?", which reminds one that Amis, despite his lack of
front-line experience, was a soldier and aware of the pressures of war.
Its last six lines could have been written by the twenty-four-year-old
James Churchill of *The Anti-Death League:*

> Noel should be here now, her giant body
> Vibrating close to mine, hiding the view;
> Her breathing drowning the guns, her smell overlaying
> The stink of the lustless dead, her naked flesh
> Bringing a shudder nothing to do with fear:
> Noel keep the war away by being with me.

A similar unprotected honesty is evident in Amis's most self-analyt-
ical poem, "Release," written as he was about to leave the army, uncertain of the future, and weighing past regimentation, past disappointments, against the need for self-realization and the possibility of hope.
Looking at some of its lines, unironic, lamely open, rhythmically awkward in their mixture of the poetic and the prosaic, it is hard to escape
the conclusion that much of Amis's later poetry, for all its increased
verbal and structural efficiency, involved some reduction in ordinary
human feeling, and that his virtual rejection of his first volume springs
from personal as well as technical embarrassment:

> My heart must say good-bye, and my heart must want;
> It is slow to learn, and nothing is any good
> If I have decided merely what not to want.
> . . . .
> I want to exchange the blow for the caress,
> And yet I am suspicious and weary. . . .

Two final poems from *Bright November* show Amis looking outward, at what he is leaving behind in war-torn Europe and at what he has returned to in postwar England. Both poems combine the mannerisms of Auden with the uneasy, dragging, more personal melancholy which sounds like a pedal-point through the volume. "Belgian Winter" observes a wrecked landscape, "the plains awkwardly revealed by history," a bewildered population "unable to understand, / Randy for cigarettes, moving hands too / Jerky to move in love," a city of "opera and lesbian exhibitions" in which "The conqueror is advised to keep to the boulevards." From this unsatisfactory and unhappy scene, "given us as the end of something / Important," the transfer to England, so looked forward to by Lieutenant Frank Archer in "I Spy Strangers," brings little pleasure. "Berkhamsted" (perhaps visited by Amis in connection with his Oxford research on Graham Greene) presents a dreary world whose emotional claustrophobia is mirrored by the poem's unusual stanza-pattern: the first and last lines of each stanza end with the same word. Amis is sensitive to the town's provincial, home counties atmosphere, its Betjemanesque externals lacking inner vitality:

> Come with me: I will show you what I mean.
> Think of this town as autumn afternoon
> Restless with leaves in Doctor's Commons Road.
> . . . .
> Follow the tall green bus to the High Street
> Past teas of cress and Marmite, rooms that face
> Unnoticed sadness of blank playing fields.

Returning to the bourgeois England which Auden had left for America in 1939, Amis finds in it the same complacency, the same resistance to change, as Auden had attacked in *The Orators* in 1932:

> In this town, stranger, think of nothing wrong:
> When England falls, look for an enclave here
> Among the randy and archaic pure,
> Always well-bred, never to know despair,
> Ardent in living at no temperature,
> Anointed with the grace of being wrong.

A slight ambivalence in Amis's description makes it understandable why, eventually, he came to align himself with conservative values; but one can also see in his picture of Berkhamsted, self-quarantined from

life or sadly isolated from it, a reason why Amis might have felt dis-
satisfied with the country he had returned to, and ready to do something that might shake it up.

II   A Case of Samples (1956)

Amis's fourth collection included two poems, already mentioned,
from *Bright November,* but also the contents of two intervening slim-
mer volumes published by small presses. The first was *A Frame of
Mind,* a limited edition issued in 1953 by the University of Reading
School of Art, and containing eighteen poems, among them "The
Value of Suffering," "Legends," and "Aiming at a Million," distinctly
Gravesian in atmosphere and technique. The other was a pamphlet
(No. 22) printed in 1954 by the Fantasy Press, outside Oxford. The
pamphlet included the interesting if rather oblique poem "Act of
Kindness" and "The Last War," an allegorical rather than a historical
poem, abounding in Audenisms like "The third owned a museum, the
fourth a remarkable gun."[10] A reviewer found the pamphlet "less distinguished" than *A Frame of Mind:* it "perhaps to some extent represents rejects from that."[11] Nevertheless, the decade since *Bright
November,* revealed in the forty or so poems in *A Case of Samples,*
represented a considerable improvement in Amis's technique.

The anonymous review I have quoted was devoted not to Amis
alone, but to a group of writers, including Philip Larkin and Donald
Davie, who had each published a Fantasy Press pamphlet. They shared
a quality which was indicated by the reviewer's choice of title: "The
Shield of Irony." His approval for the high general level of "rhetorical
discipline" demonstrated by Amis and the others was tempered by a
caveat which their tendency to irony, to a wary skirting of personal
involvement, prompted: a worry whether "the setting . . . of old heads
on young shoulders may not also sometimes have the effect of wither-
ing young hearts." In the attempt to impose a "rhetorical discipline"
and an orderly expression on events and feelings, irony and its dangers
were occupational risks accepted more or less willingly by Amis and
the other eight poets (including Davie and Larkin) who appeared in a
volume published the same year as *A Case of Samples:* the anthology
New Lines (1956), which, put together and polemically introduced by
Robert Conquest, expressed the anti-Romantic sentiments of "the
Movement," as the poets published in it came to be known. Sensibly,
Conquest did not insist on yoking together too strongly nine poets who
in many respects differed from one another (and were to diverge on

even more individual paths in later years); but they did, he felt, have one important thing, if a negative one, in common: a "determination to avoid bad principles."[12]

Putting this more positively, and in a way which certainly applies to Amis, one may say that the Movement poets shared two watchwords: strictness of form, and clarity of expression; and it was in the context of *New Lines* that Amis first became widely known as a poet. His own doubts about romanticism are stated, persuasively, in "Against Romanticism," one of nine poems (also in *A Case of Samples*) anthologized there, but the sharpness of his hostility to one of its most famous contemporary practitioners, Dylan Thomas, is evident from the only poem in *A Case of Samples* which he chose not to reprint in his *Collected Poems*. Dylan Thomas had died in 1953; Amis's "A Poet's Epitaph" is a three-line, acid engraving:

> They call you "drunk with words"; but when we drink
> And fetch it up, we sluice it down the sink.
> You should have stuck to spewing beer, not ink.

This honest, if ungracious, comment carries an extra charge of self-rejection. It takes one to know one, and as this stanza from "Something Was Moaning in a Corner," a *Bright November* poem of before 1943, makes plain, Amis himself, like so many young poets, had once suffered from "the D.T.'s":

> O viper, mad with coiling on a pin,
> Deadly Narcissus gazing on your scales,
> Vomit your naked young sentenced to pain
> And learn to love the bad sun where it scalds.

Amis's rejection of Dylan Thomas (and George Barker) was stated more quietly, in terms of a general shift in poetic fashion, in a slightly earlier anthology which, coincidentally, contained all the poets who appeared in *New Lines*, with the exception of Thom Gunn. This was *Poets of the 1950's*, published in Tokyo in 1955[13] and edited by D. J. Enright. It included statements by each of the poets about the kind of poetry they wrote, and what they thought poetry ought to do. Amis made it clear that, for him, poetry is essentially a form of public communication, not an excuse for private self-indulgence, and that the individual poem—rather than a mystical, capitalized entity called "Poetry"—is the root of the matter: "Every poem is an attempt at solving a completely new problem." Technique is clearly crucial, too. Amis stated that whenever "a new poem looks like getting itself written" he bore in mind two needs: the need for the poem to interest others as well as himself, and his own need to avoid staleness by "working it into a verse form I haven't used before, or at any rate not recently."[14]

A few poems from A *Case of Samples* which show Amis's own emerging voice rather than Auden's or Graves's may serve to illustrate his technical skill, his attitudes and their possible limitations, and also, on occasion, his humor—usually mocking, whether directed at others or at himself. "Something Nasty in the Bookshop,"[15] sharply observant of the minimal space poetry occupies on the shelves of provincial bookshops and wry about poetic competitiveness, is concerned to contrast, via their titles, the poetic worlds of young men and women poets, the latter concerned with personal love, the former with literary showing-off. Amis makes plain enough the kind of subject matter he thinks poetry can do without:

> *Landscape near Parma*
> Interests a man, so does *The Double Vortex,*
> So does *Rilke and Buddha.*
>
> "I travel," you see, "I think" and "I can read"
> These titles seem to say.

At the same time, as his conclusion makes plain, he is not at all sure whether poems that say "I feel" or "I love" are to be preferred. At least, he cannot write them, and conveys his uncertainty in a witty "metaphysical" hyperbole:

> Should poets bicycle-pump the human heart
> Or squash it flat?

G. S. Fraser once described the Movement's "ideal" poem as a set of particulars (a described scene or incident) which swung via interior reflection toward some sort of intellectual conclusion.[16] "Something Nasty" follows this paradigm exactly, its central stanza providing the pivot:

> From somewhere in this (as in any) matter
> A moral beckons.

To state a situation and then point a moral is characteristic of what I should call "middle-period" Amis (c. 1950–1967), and the same procedure is followed by "Nocturne," whose initial picture of lovers writhing in a shop-doorway and a drunken sailor yawing about "with an empty beer-flagon" turns up slightly altered in Chapter 12 of *Take a Girl like You*.[17] Such a scene, Amis suggests, would prompt "the Watch Committee" and himself to call both lovers and sailor "*Mere animals*"; but on reflection (a rather obvious one), their behavior is seen as "Nothing so sure and economical"—an ironic negative—and finally as something more positive. Amis's colloquial adjectives refer neatly to the three people, and in the penultimate line he slips in a sly reference to Yeats's "The Second Coming":

> These keep the image of another creature
> In crippled versions, cocky, drab and stewed:
> What beast holds off its paw to gesture,
> Or gropes towards being understood?

In both poems, the first more flippant, the second more serious, Amis is uneasily aware of the claims of human emotion while holding back from full endorsement of it. Amis's classic general poem on the subject is "Against Romanticism," which cleverly prevents the build-up of rhythmic eloquence (and so, perhaps, a subversion of its thesis) by alternating iambic pentameters with lines that are basically trochaic, arranged usually in two groups of five syllables:

> A traveller who walks a temperate zone
> —Woods devoid of beasts, roads that please the foot—
> Finds that its decent surface grows too thin:
> Something unperceived fumbles at his nerves.

Order and rationality ("real time and place," for Amis) become boring and drive man to more exciting visions of a life which, paradoxically, would if attained make such visions unnecessary; since it appears that visions are necessary (or at any rate unavoidable), they had best, in Amis's view, be kept simple:

> Let mine be pallid, so that it cannot
>   Force a single glance, form a single word;
>   . . . .
>   Not long, voluble swooning wilderness,
> And green, not parched or soured by frantic suns
>   Doubling the commands of a rout of gods,
> Nor trampled by the drivelling unicorn.

Whether, when men are "raging to build a better time and place /
Than the ones which give prophecy its field / To work, the calm
material for its rage," they envisage anything in their "grand meaning" as extreme as unicorns, frantic suns, and a rout of gods is debate-
able, but at least Amis's admission than "an ingrown taste for anarchy"
exists and "flaw[s] the surface that it cannot break" makes one able to
accept, in broad terms, his own preference in this poem for "plain
images . . . / Within the fingers' reach."

As a dislike of affectation characterizes Amis's novels, so the poems
of *A Case of Samples* tend to pride themselves on an uncomfortable
honesty, an unwillingness to exaggerate the real strength of emotions,
or to be taken in by stock attitudes. Nevertheless, stuck between the
"pallid" world which intellectual self-respect should prefer and tempting dreams which are liable to inflate and blow up in one's face, Amis
retains a humorous willingness to concede the force of one particular
hankering, the erotic. Two of the best, most relaxed, and technically
satisfying poems in *A Case of Samples* show Amis as the "homme
moyen sensuel," extending tolerance to dreams of sexual conquest in
"A Dream of Fair Women" and good-natured envy to the (real or
imaginary?) traveling salesman of "A Song of Experience" who regales
others with tales of the real thing. "A Dream of Fair Women" (its contents, in effect, a modern burlesque of Tennyson's poem of that name)
presents Amis himself as mobbed by a "squadron of draped nudes":

> Each girl presses on me her share of what
> Makes up the barn-door target of desire:
>   And I am a crack shot.
> Speech fails them, amorous, but each one's look,
> Endorsed in other ways, begs me to sign
>   Her body's autograph-book;
> "Me first, Kingsley; I'm cleverest" each declares. . . .

This is "all a dream," of course; but for Amis, the moral beckons that
such a dream constitutes in most men what they would wish as a reality, above all else, if they could have it:

> Who would choose any workable ideal
> In here and now's giant circumference
>   If that small room were real?
> Only the best. . . .

For the others, sadly, no doubt, "love's ordinary distances," the boring bother of real relationships, are too much, and such idealism as they have fuels repeated visits to "The halls of theoretical delight."

"A Song of Experience" reaches a similar valuation of love/lust, though since the former sex objects are changed here into "the female and the human heart" it is both jauntier and easier to concur in. Little can compare with the manifold encounters spoken of by the "dark-eyed traveller" for whom—in a phrase reminiscent of Gravesian myth-poetry—"Nausicaa and Circe were the same." He has done "What Blake presaged, what Lawrence took a stand on, / What Yeats locked up in fable," and so:

> What counter-images, what cold abstraction
>   Could start to quench that living element,
> The flash of prophecy, the glare of action?
>   —He drained his liquor, paid his score, and went.
>
> I saw him, brisk in May, in Juliet's weather,
>   Hitch up the trousers of his long-tailed suit,
> Polish his windscreen with a chamois-leather,
>   And stow his case of samples in the boot.

If a commercial traveler is hardly an exalted persona for the poet of *A Case of Samples* to adopt, there is something in the fluency of this last stanza that suggests the unironic reconciliation, admittedly on a modest level, of the claims of imagination and emotion with the earthly limits of the world which Amis prefers most of his poetry to inhabit. It is, of course, very much a man's world.

III   A Look Round the Estate (1967)

Donald Davie, writing in 1972 in *Thomas Hardy and British Poetry*, described Amis's sixth collection as "deplorable,"[18] liking in it only one poem, the political fable "After Goliath." In *A Look Round the Estate* Davie detected an element of self-pity, an unnecessary hostility to God, and an aggressive recommendation of philistine provinciality, the latter evident in the sequence "The Evans Country," the first six of whose poems had previously been published as a Fantasy Press pamphlet in 1962. Davie's judgment is difficult to accept, especially as "The Evans Country" sequence is anticipated by some of the poems I have already dealt with, so that Amis's attitude should have provoked little surprise. The self-pity (admittedly too crude in "A Chromatic Passing-Note," which Davie dislikes) and the slight broadening of Amis's outlook implied by his poems about God ("The Huge Artifice" and "New Approach Needed") seem to me symptomatic of a necessary movement, effected perhaps by growing older, beyond the two superficially contrasting elements in *A Case of Samples:* its sometimes niggling academic rationality, and its man-in-the-street hedonism. The result, I think, is a more approachable and interesting volume: the poems are rarely powerful, but they begin to have that individuality which Amis had achieved already in fiction.

The "estate" which Amis looks round in this volume—containing only thirty-one poems, which cover the decade since 1956—is not a country estate; rather (though not in high-flown terms) it is the "estate of man" and (though his hero, Dai Evans, actually lives in a middle-class suburban house and drives a Humber car) the housing-estate cultural mentality of "The Evans Country," the same Aberdarcy as John Lewis lives in. In part, the twelve poems which make up the sequence, "Dedicated to the Patrons and Staff of the Newton Inn, Mumbles, Swansea," are an affectionately satirical record of the place Amis lived in from 1949 to 1961, in part a comic celebration of the irrepressible lusts of a married Welsh businessman of outwardly "chapel" respectability.

Ten lively vignettes, all in different stanza forms, of Dai's amatory interests and affairs—watching schoolgirls across the road from his home, burning superannuated sexy magazines in order to create "house-room" for "the real hot stuff," trying to get off with a girl on the beach, judging a beauty competition,[19] ringing up another girl after his father's Bethesda chapel funeral—are framed by two poems both in pentameter quatrains, whose purpose is to challenge the reader to question his own assumptions of superiority, which are likely to be aroused by the intervening depiction of Dai's relentless pursuit of "one thing," comic though much of it is. The first, "Aberdarcy: The Main Square," describes the progress of Dai's guilty affair with "Mrs. Rhys" in terms of its background—ugly, tasteless town center, "a lousy weekend in Porthcawl"[20]—and makes the claim that a well-adjusted relationship exists between people's feelings and their surroundings. Neither of these, here, is fancy, but both are real, and suit each other, and if Dai and Mrs. Rhys would look out of place against the architectural beauties of Venice or the cool splendors of Regency London, their situation is not for that reason, Amis insinuates, inferior to the experience of most readers:

> But how disparage what so well reflects
> Permanent tendencies of heart and mind?
>
> All love demands a witness: something "there"
> Which it yet makes part of itself. These two
> Might find Carlton House Terrace, St. Mark's Square
> A bit on the grand side. How about you?

The same question, mocking the reader's wish to find in art what life rarely provides, concludes the last poem. Dai may rush from his pub, by way of "A fearsome thrash with Mrs. No-holds-barred" to the domestic comforts of haddock, tea, and an evening in front of the television ("Aberdarcy: The Chaucer Road"), but "Who's doing better, then? How about you?" Even if one is, or thinks one is, Amis's engaging, unheroic survey of lower-middle-class mores (almost a mininovel) should induce at least a degree of tolerance: Dai's behavior is the lowest common denominator of humanity.

Some of Amis's poems in *A Look Round the Estate* express various dissatisfactions with art appropriate in a writer who distrusts the highflown. "Larger Truth" criticizes (in terms of Swansea) the novelist's search for meaning through fictional categorization and over-simplification, then turns the poet's criticism on himself:

> It takes a poet to be more dishonest,
> To pick stuff like this for his harangue,
> To pretend that finding or withholding meaning
>   Means anything.

"The Huge Artifice" asserts that life itself has no recognizable meaning: "*what it's all about* . . . remains in doubt." The poem, in rhyming couplets, is presented as if it were a Leavisite critic's review of some enormous novel, full of "casual meetings, parties, fights and such," and what gradually emerges is that God is the novelist criticized for "authorial inexperience." This is manifested in such nasty concepts as the advantages of indifference over love, the nonpunishment or overpunishment of crime, the destruction of "the gentle." There is no meaning in all this that Amis can see (the Amis of *The Anti-Death League*, evidently); all that is visible is "An inhumanity beyond despair."

The unsatisfactoriness of Christ's incarnation is argued in the following poem, "New Approach Needed," which is written in a kind of syllabic meter (six syllables per line, but with flexible colloquial rhythms, constantly changing). Christ did not stay long enough to "get to know the place," experience "hunger, / Madness, disease and war," or the smaller pains risked by a married man (one assumes the poem coincided with the break-up of Amis's first marriage); nor was the crucifixion, though unpleasant enough, as bad as some of the "more durable wrongs" a full lifetime entails. Unlike Christ, man (man in Amis's image, anyway) is not sustained by the certainty of immortality or by the "nice, cheering thought" that his sacrifice is not in vain:

> So, next time, come off it[21]
> And get some service in,
> Jack, long before you start
> Laying down the old law:
> If you still want to then.
> Tell your dad that from me.

How much dissatisfaction with, or sadness in, his own life lies behind Amis's "old soldier" manner to God and his impatience with theological niceties (Christ never did lay down "the old law") is suggested by three poems that reflect in various ways Amis's entry into middle age. "After Goliath" presents Amis's disillusion in political terms. The poem grafts onto its fable, in which the issue of right versus might seemed quite definite, the less clear-cut contemporary opposition between figures of "Establishment" authority such as

> . . . aldermen, adjutants, aunts,
> Administrators of grants,

and

> Angst-pushes, adherents of Zen,
> Alastors, Austenites, A-test
> Abolishers

—all the "liberal" types on whose side Amis/David sees with some dismay he has aligned himself. For Amis, indeed for any writer whose view of society is eclectic rather than narrowly ideological, the problem is that

> even the straightest
> Of issues looks pretty oblique
> When a movement turns into a clique.

Having killed his Goliath, Amis wonders whether he likes those who are cheering his victory; has the left-winger, in fact, killed "the right man"? The witty alphabetic fable encapsulates his progress from the left-wing halfheartedness of *Socialism and the Intellectuals* (1957) to the right-wing halfheartedness of *Lucky Jim's Politics* (1967).

The ageing of the philanderer (one of Amis's *personae*) is presented in "Nothing to Fear," which provides a poetic version of Patrick Standish's sudden experience of the terror of death while he waits for Jenny to turn up at his flat *(Take a Girl like You*, Ch. 23). The 'lucky sod', feeling no 'guilt, compunction and such stuff', 'nor fear of failure, thank you, Jack', is suddenly assailed by the frightening intimations of mortality, by thoughts of a situation in which he, not the girl, will become the victim of carnal concupiscence:

> . . . . it's a dead coincidence
> That sitting here, a bag of glands
> Tuned up to concert pitch, I seem to sense
> A different style of caller at my back,
> As cold as ice, but just as set on me.

The thought of death, said to arrive at 30, sharpens on the death of a parent: oneself is next. On April 18th, 1963, two days after Amis's forty-first birthday, his father died, and the most moving poem in *A Look Round the Estate* is "In Memoriam W. R. A.," in which Amis's memories of his father are triggered off by an old-fashioned cricket match in which Amis took part. Amis's plain statements are made in a careful, syllabic meter which deliberately avoids the rhythmic generation of plangent feeling, but the restrained stanzas communicate a genuine regret, moving from recollections of a shared passion for cricket to a sadder realization of their estrangements on other matters, "silence, / And separate ways." The last stanza, with its sense of "too late" and "nevermore," seems also to communicate, in addition to private apology, the suspicion of the ironist that his cast of mind may

often have prevented him from recognizing important, ordinary
emotions:

> Forgive me if I have
> To see it as it happened:
> Even your pride and your love
> Have taken this time to become
> Clear, to arouse my love.
> I'm sorry you had to die
> To make me sorry
> You're not here now.

IV   Collected Poems *(1944–1979)*

Twenty-three new poems[22] written since 1967 appear in Amis's final
volume to date, which collects most of Amis's previously published
poetry. All but one are concerned with England, and their manner is
bleak, a bleakness on the one hand palely warmed by nostalgia and on
the other jaundiced by dislike of the present and fear of a future which
threatens to be Russia-dominated ("Crisis Song") and will in any case
bring death (too many poems to list). Amis's Janus-faced outlook elsewhere is prepared for by the jaunty stoicism of "Ode to Me," written
for his fiftieth birthday in 1972. Looking round, Amis is sorry for others
with "fifty or so / Actual years to go," since they will either suffer the
rigors of Soviet rule or have become so unmanned by the decay of the
English language and "a whole generation / Of phasing out education"
that they won't notice it. Amis is glad enough, in terms of quality of
life, to look forward to "not all that many" years ahead.

At least, he would be if it were not for the thought of actual physical
death, and of the horrors of old age (evoked by the false gaiety of
"Drinking Song" and, much more powerfully, in the poem "Nicely,"
a savagely ironic "scenario" rather in the manner of D. J. Enright).
Amis's dislike (as intense as Douglas Yandell's and Jake Richardson's)
of the sights of the modern world and the mores of modern youth is
communicated with venomous brevity in "Shitty," but the real point
of this poem, driven home by the literal / colloquial meanings of the
word "sight," is the sting in its tail:

> Look thy last on all things shitty
> While thou'rt at it: soccer stars,

Soccer crowds, bedizened bushheads
　　Jerking over their guitars. . . .
. . . .
High-rise blocks and action paintings,
　　Sculptures made from wire and lead:
Each of them a sight more lovely
　　Than the screens around your bed.

Toward the end of his long army recollection, "A Reunion," Amis
recalls the days when

We were not so much young as new,
With some shine still on us, unmarked
(At least only mildly frayed),
When everything in us worked,
And no allowances made.

and in "Ode to Me" he speaks of having grown up in "a world worth
looking at twice." His poems about the present are good, angry verse;
his late poems about the past have the deeper, more evocative quality
one associates with poetry, and are among his best work, however
strangely his nostalgia rings when contrasted with the poems he
actually wrote when he was younger, poems which rarely communicate a sense of innocent, lyrical happiness. Amis's nostalgia is the late-
flowering appreciation of pleasures less than fully savored when they
were fresh, rather than the mellow memory of things once enjoyed. In
that way, he differs from John Betjeman, to whom Collected Poems
is dedicated and whose style influences some of the nostalgic late
poems in it; but just as the "genre" element in some of his novels allows
him to speak without irony, so the pioneer work of Betjeman in evoking the London suburbs and 1920s Oxford gives him a kind of mask
behind which he can speak with an unembarrassed emotion which is
the more accomplished resurgence of the halting young poet of Bright
November.

The foci of nostalgic regret in the three Betjeman-influenced poems
are Amis's childhood, his university days, and his early (and lasting)
enthusiasm for the heyday of jazz and its "greats." "Bobby Bailey"
hardly needs commenting on here; I have spoken of it in Chapter 1
and in relation to The Riverside Villas Murder. "Their Oxford"[23] is
more complex in its retrospect, the work of a Jake Richardson who,
though equally hostile to the present, is more honest about the past he

commemorates. The poem's densely packed quatrains work up a strong emotion, anger at contemporary "town" Oxford in Part I, a sonorous regret for the loss of Amis's own "gown" Oxford, not fully appreciated at the time, in Part II. The past, for Amis, had more *character* than the present—the Roebuck was a pub

> Where men in long top-coats would snort and scratch,
> Meat-market porters gulp their morning break,
> And stall-boys jostle; now, yards off, you catch
> The surge and the thunder of a discothèque.

—instead of "the surge and thunder of the Odyssey" celebrated by the Oxford don Andrew Lang in his famous sonnet. Part II turns from the commercialized modern town to the contemplation of Oxford University's former glories, academic and social:

> In my day there were giants on the scene,
> Men big enough to be worth laughing at:
> Coghill and Bowra, Lewis and Tolkien.
> Lost confidence and envy finished that.
> . . . .
> Do costly girls still throng the chequered lawn,
> All bosom and bright hair, as they did then,
> And laugh and dance and chatter until dawn
> With peacock-minded, donkey-voiced young men?

Having come in at the tail end of it, and having (one is allowed to infer) not been entirely at home there, Amis frankly calls the place "that Oxford that I hardly knew." The envy of his own generation was partly what helped it to decline, as he is honest enough to admit, but now he is sorry to record its passing, seeing it not as just a set of romantically falsified memories but as a period intrinsically richer and better than what has replaced it:

> With mildly coveting what I could see
> Went disapproval, but at this remove,
> When no one here cares how it used to be
> Except the old, how can I disapprove?
>
> What seemed to me so various is all one,
> A block of time, which like its likenesses

> Looks better now the next such has begun;
> Looks, and in this case maybe really is.

The last sizable poem in the volume is "Farewell Blues," a lament for the passing of all the jazz musicians whom Amis learned to love in his youth, and so many of whose records, with their "Brunswick," "Decca," and "Okeh" labels, are now deleted. For Amis, the unfamiliar instruments, the academic jazz, the oddly named "groups" that have replaced them, are so much "bloody row."

To underscore the sense of a lost tradition which his own preferences express Amis casts his blues into the form used by John Betjeman for his poem "Dorset,"[24] whose changing refrain, a list of literary and euphonious names, is itself modeled on the opening and closing lines of Thomas Hardy's nostalgic poem "Friends Beyond."[25] In the first two stanzas, the names of Amis's idols swing like bells to drown out the uncongenial noises of the present—the "Trumpets gelded, drums contingent, saxophones that bleat and bawl." In the last his conservative sorrow for their fading takes over completely and becomes an angry elegy for everything—youth, emotional innocence, wonder—that is worn away by the passage of time:

> Dead's the note we loved that sang within us, made us
>   gasp and stare,
> Simple joy and simple sadness thrashing the astounded air;
> What replaced them no one asked for, but it turned up
>   anyhow,
> And Coleman Hawkins, Johnny Hodges, Bessie Smith and
>   Pee Wee Russell lie in Okeh churchyard now.

Amis's poetic achievement as a whole—intellectually interesting and technically versatile, if limited in its emotional reach and imaginative horizons—entitles him to the status of a good minor poet. In some of these late poems, at least, he reveals the potential to be more than that.

CHAPTER 9

Other Fiction

AFTER he retired from university teaching in 1963, moved to London, and took up the life of the professional writer, Amis continued to produce novels at much the same rate as before, but his output of poetry declined to a trickle. Instead he increasingly occupied himself with various levels of nonfiction. One level was the approachably academic: essays and reviews, two anthologies of poetry, a pictorial biography of Rudyard Kipling; another was middlebrow: a book on drink, a book investigating the phenomenon (much enjoyed by Amis) of Ian Fleming's James Bond novels—*The James Bond Dossier;* the third was public and political: his collection of material from the period when the Labour politician Harold Wilson was Prime Minister *(Harold's Years)* and his satirical contributions to the *Black Papers,* collections of criticism directed at left-wing educational theories and the consequent decline in quality of postwar British state education.

In this chapter I am concerned only with the rest of his creative work. Two further novels deserve only brief mention: *The Egyptologists* (1965), written in collaboration with Robert Conquest, and *Colonel Sun* (1968), Amis's revival of James Bond in an anti-Chinese setting, which he published under the pen name Robert Markham. Of the latter, since whatever Amis's ingenuity in creating colorful settings and an exciting plot the character used is Ian Fleming's, little relevant to Amis's peculiar abilities as a novelist can be said: the object of the exercise was to create a satisfactory facsimile of a James Bond novel by means of a ventriloquial exercise in genre-writing, and this, to my mind, Amis succeeds in doing.

Since *The Egyptologists* was a collaboration, not much can usefully be said of it, either, though Amis makes something possible as a result of having indicated in an interview roughly the extent of his involvement.[1] The original idea and draft were Robert Conquest's, as was "a lot of the dialogue, the science fiction dream, the Nefertiti statue"; Amis was responsible for the plot, the introduction of the women (the

132

club-members' wives and Lee Eddington Schwartz, the American girl
who is interested in the club's activities), and the television debacle in
Chapter 18. The occurrence of an offstage professor called L. Stone
Caton can also with confidence be attributed to Amis.

Much of *The Egyptologists*—which begins with the sentence
"Their lives were built on caution"—is mystification for its own sake,
challenging the reader to work out what, in reality, the members of
this quasi-esoteric London society are up to: it is a kind of spoof pre-
figuring of the "security" element in *The Anti-Death League*. The
"Metropolitan Egyptological Society" is, in fact, a group of men who
simply wish to escape from their wives: they are devoted to what the
secretary, in Chapter 17, calls "the cause of virism," and one may think
of the novel as a sympathetic joke at the expense of the whole "club-
man" mentality. The treatment of the men versus women theme is
light, but Cambuslang's discovery (Ch. 16) that "women are the trouble, not marriage after all," may contain the seed, fifteen years earlier,
of *Jake's Thing*. In Chapter 18, the hilarious but potentially fatal scene
in which the Egyptologists are challenged on television by a real expert
in the subject, one may also discern an element which came to more
serious fruition in the Ronnie Appleyard of *I Like It Here*—the TV
interviewer Eric Lasker, who possesses "that humble unpretentious
insincerity which had endeared him to countless homes."

More serious and more important are Amis's short stories; there are
sixteen of these, and among them are some of Amis's most considerable
pieces of writing, a body of work with which a study of his literary
career may properly conclude.

I My Enemy's Enemy *(1962)*

Kingsley Amis does not regard himself as fictionally ambidextrous:
for him, his short stories are essentially "something too short to be
called a novel . . . an idea which is suitable for narrative and which
cannot be stretched to the length of a novel."[2] Consequently he has
produced few of them; but those few display a fine instinct for com-
pleteness within a limited space, together with a control of tone and a
sobriety of expression, which is impressive and remarkable. They are
an underrated part of his achievement in prose fiction.

My Enemy's Enemy, his only collection, brings together seven stories, of which six had already appeared in magazines between 1955
and 1962. "Something Strange" (1960), a chilly study of psychological

conditioning through isolation, is presented in the guise of science fiction; its conclusion, in which Bruno, a more imaginative character than the rest, brings Myri out of her catatonia by telling her he loves her, anticipates in reverse the situation of Catherine and James Churchill in *The Anti-Death League*.

The other stories are set in more recognizable worlds, two of them in the Aberdarcy of *That Uncertain Feeling*. The less important of these is "Interesting Things" (1956), which describes the evening spent by Gloria Davies, an eighteen-year-old comptometer operator (and putative sister of Ken Davies?), in the company of Mr. Huws-Jones, an income-tax inspector who harbors romantic longings under a boring and untrendy exterior. The story is an economical, ironic study of cultural dismay and noncommunication, a dry run for parts of *Take a Girl like You*.

"Moral Fibre" (1958) is twice as long, and both morally and politically penetrating; it also presents a John Lewis who is far happier at home than in *That Uncertain Feeling*, and far less flippant, while still being recognizably the same character. The story is concerned with four phases in John Lewis's observation, through his acquaintance with the social worker Mair Webster, of the life of Betty Arnulfsen, a delinquent young woman who in his view is not "really fallen, just rather inadmissibly inclined from the perpendicular." In Mair's opinion, Betty merely drifts through life and lacks "moral fibre": she is a case requiring treatment, and receiving a species of bluff kindness and condescension. To John, seeing her first as a rather downtrodden cleaning-woman, then as a prosperous prostitute, immoral but "free," and later as a reformed housewife, moral but "tamed," she is a human being looking for some sort of tolerable life.

Sufficient admiration of Mair is conveyed to stop the story from being unfair: John sees that "on the face of it Mair had a claim to be considered the less disreputable character, up there in the firing line while cowards flinched and traitors sneered." This theoretical admiration, however, is outweighed by John's dislike of the bossy personal attitudes involved in such a job, attitudes which, though a conscientious Socialist, he sees as the less acceptable face of socialism itself: "off the face of it . . . the picture changed a bit, just as things like the Labour Party looked better from some way away than close to." Nevertheless, though the human sympathies of the story lie with Betty, she is not sentimentalized: when she eventually "breaks out" and receives a jail sentence for burglary, it is Mair who speaks for her and visits her, and though Mair's sort can be criticized, the problem of Betty remains. Amis looks shrewdly and realistically at the difficulty of reconciling the individuality and freedom of real if erratic people with the demands of social responsibility and order.

Authority, who wields it and how, is among the matters treated in Amis's "two stories and a novella" about army life in Belgium at the end of World War II. The three pieces, linked by recurrent characters, convey the small tensions and the overarching boredom of life in non-combatant units of the Royal Signals with great authenticity, and taken together their eighty-four pages are virtually a short novel, moving forward from the last year of war into the first year of peace and the establishment of the postwar Labour government.

The first story, "My Enemy's Enemy" (1955), is narrated in the third person but seen mostly from the viewpoint of Captain Tom Thurston, who, with his Oxford degree and his interest in literary magazines, seems a partial and senior surrogate for Amis himself. Essentially, the story is about moral responsibility and personal loyalty, and what it suggests, strongly enough, is the limitations of the intellectual outlook, in which thinking and talk serve as substitutes for action. Thurston's problem of loyalty is created when the ex–Territorial Army adjutant reveals his hostility to Lieutenant Dalessio,[3] an efficient technical officer but quite unconcerned about military discipline and smartness. Thurston defends Dalessio, but when a snap inspection threatens to land him and his sloppy line-maintenance billet in trouble, Thurston does nothing to warn him about it, being afraid that the adjutant will make his own life awkward if he does.

Instead, the warning is given by Captain Bentham, a Regular Officer risen from the ranks whom the educated Thurston rather looks down on. Bentham dislikes Dalessio's unmilitary slovenliness, but dislikes even more the "ignorant jumped-up so-called bloody gentlemen from the Territorial Army" who are out to get him, and sharply reproaches Thurston at the end for his lack of moral courage and simple decency. The reproof is fully deserved, and leaves Thurston with nothing to say, though learning no doubt that Bentham is at least his friend in the sense of being his enemy's enemy. The story presents a well-observed gallery of army types, and adumbrates, in its opposition of technical efficiency and the military mystique, the class-war theme which emerges in "I Spy Strangers."

The central story, "Court of Inquiry" (1956), forms a bitter little interlude, told in the first person by Captain Jock Watson. Set in 1944, it describes from his incredulous point of view the unnecessary court of inquiry set up by the would-be martinet Major Raleigh in response to the loss of an obsolete charging engine by a young, accident-prone subaltern, Frank Archer. What could easily have been victimization is neutralized by Archer's skill in making a great parade of abject apology to Raleigh, in acting, in fact, "like a hysterical schoolgirl." Archer (like Amis, his original[4]) is a "good mimic," and though Watson himself is not entirely sure "whether any amount of acting talent could have produced the blushes I had seen," the final impression one is left with is that Archer has made a fool of Raleigh and the bureaucratic nonsense he represents. The army has, in fact, "made a man" of him, teaching him not the virtues of courage but the advantages of low cunning.

The third army story, Amis's longest, is his novella "I Spy Strangers." Previously unpublished, and so presumably dating from not much earlier than 1962, it is set in North Germany just after the surrender and on the eve of the British election that ousted Winston Churchill and installed a Labour government. Previously mentioned officers like Dalessio, Thurston, and Watson have been posted to Potsdam, while Major Raleigh is left in charge of a unit with little to do but stage mock-Parliamentary debates, with one of which the story opens.

Raleigh, a conservative and a military romantic, who hopes vainly for promotion and for the postwar continuance of the middle-class, established England to which he belongs, senses in his unit's strongly felt debates the emergence of a new and uncongenial spirit:

Something monstrous and indefinable was growing in strength, something hostile to his accent and taste in clothes and modest directorship and ambitions for his sons and redbrick house at Purley with its back-garden tennis court.[5]

This spirit is particularly evident in Frank Archer and in one of the soldiers in his section, a signalman called Hargreaves, who comes into conflict not initially with Raleigh but with Doll, the orderly-room sergeant who resembles Bentham in "My Enemy's Enemy." Looking at the postwar situation in Europe from the military point of view, Doll sees the victorious Russians, and the Communist principles they stand for, as the political enemies of Britain in the future. Hargreaves, though no Communist, has such strong left-wing class loyalties, bred in the 1930s, that he sees Doll's position as neo-Fascist and denounces it in words which call to mind Auden's influence on the poetry Amis was writing at the end of the war:

I know your sort, Doll. There are people like you in England, all over, in the bloody empire, Africa and India, smooth as buggery in the club with the old brandy and soda and then off to break a strike or flog a wog. . . . You're going to lose. You're on the side of death. History'll get you. Auden warned you but you never listened.

But it is Doll, in fact, who ameliorates the fate that Hargreaves calls down on himself later, after another debate in which the future of England under a Labour government is described by its advocates. This will involve either abolishing "the public schools and Oxford and Cambridge" or opening them up to all people with brains, reducing the power of the House of Lords and the Monarchy, and giving the country "to the ordinary working bloke and by Christ he's going to be running things from now on." Unable to keep from intervening, Major Raleigh, sitting in the "visitors' gallery," rises to praise the virtues of the stratified England he prefers:

. . . it would be an awful pity if we were to let one another down by forgetting the things that have made it all [the British victory] possible, the teamwork and sense of responsibility, and behind that the way of life we're been fighting for. We've always been a pretty good-natured lot, we British, and the fellow up there . . . and the fellows down there . . . have always got on pretty well together.

This dose of platitudes provokes in the intransigent Hargreaves the objection: "I Spy Strangers," the Parliamentary formula which calls for the visitors' gallery to be cleared, and despite the embarrassment of Frank Archer as Speaker, Major Raleigh has no option but to leave. As Hargreaves's and Archer's commanding officer, Raleigh takes advantage of his position to put both of them on a troop draft to the unfinished war in the Far East, seeing himself as purging the unit of undesirable elements. Doll, though himself intending to turn his back on a Socialist England by emigrating to Kenya or Rhodesia, adds to the draft list Hargreaves's close friend Signalman Hammond, thus effectively counteracting Raleigh's vindictiveness. Archer himself is saved from his fate by being released early from his wartime service in order to resume his studies at Oxford.

The end of the story shows Raleigh swallowing his disappointment at not becoming a colonel, together with the unwelcome news that his home constituency has gone over to the left by an enormous margin in the election. Yet Amis's story, perhaps because it was written so many years after the situation it describes, is far from leaving the reader entirely pleased by Raleigh's discomfiture; its virtue is its fairness to the wide range of English types involved in the end-of-war political shift: the idealistic Socialist Hargreaves, the hopeful democrat Archer, the old-fashioned hierarchy-respecting Doll, the entrenched and rather pathetic Conservative Major Raleigh. The last word, uttered from Raleigh's viewpoint, is by no means a merely ironic sample of hopeless Tory nostalgia, anticipating as it does Amis's own swing during the 1960s from the left to the right:

But the world was wide. . . . Much of what he believed in must survive.
    And the guarantee of that was England. England had been up against it in 1940, in 1914, and no doubt earlier, with the Napoleon business and so on. . . . All that was needed was faith. Despite everything that Hargreaves and Archer and the rest of them might do, England would muddle through somehow.

The need, or at least the wish, for faith of a different kind, not patriotic but religious, is a key element in Amis's most moving story, "All the Blood within Me" (1962). The title is a phrase from Longfellow's "Hiawatha," occurring in what was once a favorite drawing-room ballad, "Onaway, Awake, Beloved," arranged as a duet with piano accompaniment by Coleridge-Taylor and other composers. The ballad perfectly crystallizes the sort of lower-middle-class restrained passion which has been felt by the story's main character, Alec Mackenzie, for a married woman, Betty Duerden, whose funeral he is setting out to attend. In a level style which moves easily from observation to feeling, from present to past, and from sharpness to sympathy, Amis presents what is essentially the whole of Alec's emotional life in terms of a single day's events and the memories they evoke, as, in a small-scale five-act procession, Alec moves through the train journey, the church service, the burial, the pub lunch afterwards, to a final conversation outside the pub which reveals his lonely present life and the possible illusoriness of the feelings which have sustained him through a long bachelor existence. Alec is sixty-four, the woman to whom he has been devoted was sixty-seven, and their intense but platonic "attachment," never acknowledged outwardly by either, is set against the prospect of death and an uncertainty about the meaning of life.

There is a touching "period" quality both in Alec's silent love for Betty, which originated in his first sight of her, in August 1929, at "the mixed doubles tournament at the tennis club near Balham we all used to belong to,"[6] and in its compatibility with Alec's close friendship with her husband, Jim (now seventy). His sense of Betty, Jim, and himself as "the Trio" (not just as an "eternal triangle") is related by Alec's memory to a prewar occasion when they sang the romantic "Hiawatha" duet and he played the accompaniment: a perfect natural symbol, to the reader, of Alec's tacit, secondary role, the incident revealed to Alec the existence of "a relationship between three people for which none of the ordinary words—friendship, love, understanding, intimacy—would quite do."

At the funeral service, doing his best in a nonchurchgoing age to speak of a woman he does not know to mourners he does not know, the rector conveys in eloquent generalizations the seriousness of death and the uniqueness of each individual life:

Elizabeth Duerden lives in those who knew her and loved her. . . . There is nobody, there never has been anybody, of whom it can be said that the world would have been the same if they had never lived.

Alec admires the sermon, whose words apply with great force to him, but cannot yet feel Betty's death with the immediacy it seems to him to deserve. Death, the rector concludes, "will always be cheated" by the illumination we receive from the life of anyone we have loved, by our own realization of "the human capacity for tenderness, for generosity, for gaiety, for disregard of self, for courage, for forgiveness, for intelligence, for compassion, for loyalty, for humility"; yet Alec is unable to pray to a "principle of good . . . existing above and beyond everything," or to imagine the dead Betty as "having a future." Without presenting the rector's words as hollow, Amis shows very clearly the gap between theological hope and everyman's difficulty in really believing. It is at the graveside, as earth is thrown onto the coffin, that Alec's mental picture of his life—"he had loved a fine woman and known a true friend"—is jolted by the physical fact of Betty's death. If there is "consolation" for the living, is there any for the dead? And is there, for that matter, any real consolation for the living?:

How did it help the *dead* to have made the living aware of certain things? What good to anyone were *ideas* about lovable qualities . . . What could you *do* when you were illuminated about human possibilities, except go around telling yourself how illuminated you were? What was *knowing* in aid of? And what was it to *have loved* someone?

What, Alec cries out, have his past thirty years—a romantic love but none of the companionship of marriage—been for? Has he wasted his life?

The latter part of the story, lowering the temperature by moving into the world of family piety, leaves the matter open. Whether "wasted" in any specific way or not, life passes, and at the pub Alec realizes how much of the furniture of his life—"the tennis club, the Liberal Association . . . keeping up with the new plays, music in the sense he understood"—is "no longer there." When Annette, Betty's daughter, reveals to Alec the less pleasant side of Betty herself—"all smiles on the surface and needling away whenever she got the chance"—together with Betty's amusement at Alec's devotion, the reader may feel that Alec's romanticism, criticized by Annette as being "the best sort [of love], the sort you don't have to do anything about or get to know the person," may have been an illusion, not sustaining him through his life but distracting him from a fuller one. Alec himself has lived too long with his point of view to be easily upset; but "he still felt as if he had spent thirty-two years preparing a gift that had had, and could conceivably have had, no recipient. . . ." Perhaps the essential sadness of the story, whose conclusion is a chastening but not a defeat, is best expressed by the simple phrase with which it ends, after Annette has suggested that Alec and her family meet more often: "It's a pity," he says, "it's such a long way." The physical distance referred to can stand equally for that between people, between imagination and "reality," between the present and the past, and between the living and the dead.

Faithful alike to human hopes and human limitations, Amis's treatment of the ordinary but profound issues presented in this short story is among his most impressive pieces of fiction. In capsule form it combines the theoretical ambitions for seriousness of *The Anti-Death League* with the social nostalgia of *The Riverside Villas Mystery;* in the subtlety of its awareness, in its ability to strike the heart, it seems to me not inferior to either. Much of its communicative force springs, I suspect, from a personal involvement not to be easily related to Amis's biography or family history but suggested by the presence in the story of elements tangentially related to both. Alec and the Duerdens once lived in nearby houses off Clapham Common; the Duerdens went to live in Buckinghamshire (just as Bobby Bailey's family "moved to a

place called Penn"); Jim (like Amis's father) has worked for his local
Ratepayers' Association; Alec occasionally has Sunday lunch at the
home of a colleague in the "export department" of an unspecified City
firm; on retirement Alec intends to join his brother's "glass merchan-
dising firm". Totally lacking in any ironies but those a sensitive reader
can perceive in its very fidelity to human behavior and social ambience, "All the Blood within Me" seems to derive from a source in Amis
himself very close to home, and like the hotel manager offering his
condolences, it speaks, without sentimentality or falsification, "the language of decent feeling."

II   Dear Illusion *(1972)*

Since *My Enemy's Enemy* Amis has published seven short stories,
the last, which appeared in the "Saturday Review" section of *The
Times*, as recently as November 1979. Entitled "The House on the
Headland" and set in Crete, this seems in some ways a spin-off from
Amis's experiments in genre-writing. Gripping as its unfolding events
are, however, and shocking as is its "horror" denouement, the story is
more interesting as a sophisticated, Maughamesque piece of storytell-
ing than involving as a human experience in any way typical.

"Dear Illusion" is another matter. Published in a limited edition of
600 copies in 1972, this is a touching but also funny story "all about an
old poet who wondered if perhaps that long lifetime of effort hadn't
been wasted. Wondered if he was really any good."[7] Since Amis himself has admitted to "a lot of doubts about Whether It's All Worth
While"[8]—the artist's endeavor, that is, rather than life itself—one may
see in the story of the poet Edward Arthur Potter some of Amis's own
uncertainties and, in addition, perhaps, his own sense of the unrelia-
bility of literary criticism as a guide to a writer's real stature.

The origin of "Dear Illusion"—whose first section, complete with
fussing photographer, updates Garnet Bowen's investigation of Wulfstan Strether in *I Like It Here*—may lie in an experience of Amis's
wife, Elizabeth Jane Howard, who, earlier in her life, had visited
Evelyn Waugh for a television interview which he would only grant
to "a beautiful young lady."[9] Sue Macnamara, who interviews Ted Potter, is "a long-legged girl of 30," and the "creaking iron gate" made of
"tall loops of iron" through which she passes into his front garden in
Kent is quite a good description of the gate of Waugh's house at
Combe Florey in Somerset, which he bought in 1956. But there seems
no model for Potter himself, a "great" but very obscure poet born in

Croydon in 1899, and all one can say of his very ordinary name is that it satirizes the romantic idea that poets should be extraordinary people.[10]

Potter emerges as a very human and sympathetic figure, though certainly a puzzling one: his tastes in literature are not so much eclectic as higgledy-piggledy, and he does little of any interest, nothing exciting, and is indifferent to his surroundings. He doubts the value of what he writes, takes no "pride in achievement," and his poetry is essentially therapeutic: a sense of total pointlessness, first experienced when he worked in a timber yard, was temporarily alleviated by writing words down, and the pattern has persisted. Now, however, he has decided to stop writing the poems which, once finished, he never reads again anyway:

From my point of view, nothing at all could compensate for getting on forty years of feeling bad with a couple of days of not feeling so bad and ten minutes of feeling all right thrown in about once a month.

For Potter, poetry really is the "mug's game" T. S. Eliot once described it as being, and he is about to embark on a course of pills which will probably take away both the need and the ability to write more poems. Between the old poet and the young reporter a restrained "tendresse" develops; before she leaves she prepares a simple meal for him to heat up later, and in return he presents her with the only copy of his last poem, entitled "Unborn": his farewell to some unspecified "Dear illusion with the bright hair"—his muse, perhaps, or as Sue surmises some "unrealised" or "unrealisable" ideal.

One matter, however, remains for Potter to clear up, and in the second part of the story he finds a solution to it which at least satisfies him by confirming his own grave doubts. Has his poetry been as good as the critics have made out? Has it been any good at all? Has he, as he suspects, wasted his life? A year after the interview he publishes, against expectation, a final volume mysteriously entitled *Off*, and Sue Macnamara finds herself invited to a celebratory dinner at which Potter is to be presented with a special prize of £1,000 to "attest his status as premier lyrist in the English language." "Unborn"—a real if modest poem, a simple idea fancied up by stylistic jaggedness—is not in the volume, whose contents, to judge by the samples Amis provides, are an odd hotchpotch: derivative, experimental, far from good, and, in Sue's view, uncharacteristic of Potter's work. Nevertheless, at the dinner, they are praised in fulsome terms, with apparent sincerity, and with no sense that they differ from Potter's earlier "distinctive and utterly individual tone of voice," by a leading critic, and the possibility, suggested by the volume's title, that Potter is giving up poetry is clearly not relished by an "enthusiastic" audience. In his polite but devastating reply, Potter states that his title is incomplete: it requires in front of it "a verb in I believe it's called the imperative. . . . Clear off would be nearly good enough." Since, as he reveals, his new "poems" were all written in a single day "in any style I thought of," any praise of them effectively negates the value of the praise given his poems in the past.

Escaping from the consternation caused by his speech and his tearing up of the check, Potter ends the evening by discussing with Sue his certainty, now, that he has "never been any good." He is quite without bitterness, either about his own knowledge or toward the critics—"a lot of silly donkeys"—who have led him astray. Later, however, Sue explains Potter's surprising suicide as a wish to apologize

for being a bad poet, for having spent most of his life doing nothing but write bad poetry, or poetry he thought he'd proved was bad, and wasting everybody's time. He wanted to show he minded.

Whether apologetic or not, Potter is at least free of the "dear illusion", apparently valuable and sustaining, which has messed up his life.

In the story's conclusion there is a similarity of idea, though not of mood, to "All the Blood within Me," even in terms of Sue's final thought as she wonders "how best to serve Potter's memory" by her as yet unpublished account of their conversation: "she felt like someone ineptly clutching a token of quite obscure significance, a gift with no recipient." Touching and only mildly satirical (Amis does not commit himself to the view that critics are necessarily fools), "Dear Illusion" offers on the human level a vividly sketched picture of two people reaching sympathetically across the generation gap: Potter himself, quirky, slightly pathetic, but also shrewd and far from negligible, is one of Amis's most interesting character studies. On a more philosophical level the story suggests the mysteriousness of life and the impulses that enable people to sustain it, and how difficult it is to be sure of the value of anything one produces, whether it be literature or literary criticism.

CHAPTER 10

An Interim Assessment

REVIEWING *Lucky Jim* in 1954, Walter Allen described Amis as "a novelist of formidable and uncomfortable talent."[1] Certainly meant as discriminating praise, these words have taken on over the last twenty-five years and twelve subsequent Amis novels a fuller resonance which now makes them perhaps the most accurate short summary of his achievement. "Formidable" in the French colloquial sense Amis's novels surely are, having almost always, by their liveliness of invention and verbal virtuosity, provoked in reviewers the equivalent of noisy applause accompanied by cries of "Terrific!" But they are also formidable in the more serious sense, offering behind their comedy (and, more recently, instead of it) a distinctly unwelcoming view of life and human behavior; Bernard Bergonzi has noted the "savage" element in Jim Dixon's fantasies about Professor Welch, and though it ignores the countervailing power of love also presented by Amis's novels there is much acuteness in his remark that "the world of Amis's fiction is basically Hobbesian, where mutual hostility is the normal relationship between the inhabitants."[2]

The "uncomfortable" nature of Amis's talent is manifested in at least three ways. His main characters are always found in (or soon find themselves in) situations which make them uncomfortable: for Jim Dixon his uncongenial job and the social environment that goes with it; for Patrick Standish his love for Jenny, which is as much an overwhelming itch as a delight; for Bernard Bastable the "false position" of old age and inevitable death. In all Amis's novels much of the interest is generated by the protagonist's maneuvers, sometimes purposeful and Houdini-like but as often an irritated St. Vitus' dance, to escape from what confines him: will he manage it, and if so, how? Such laughter as his contortions provoke is more and more often on the other side of the reader's face; but the reader is also made uncomfortable by Amis's sharp eye for the people and situations he chooses to depict—in Bergonzi's view, Amis's "principal strength as a novelist" is his

144

"marvellous accuracy of social observation,"[3] but the mirror he holds up is not a flattering one. Nor does it present a total human picture; to mention just one omission (an important one in a writer so apparently interested in male-female relationships), the reader may well feel discomfort at never seeing in it the reflection of a woman who combines culture, intelligence, and sexual attraction.

But in addition to the discomforts it creates for his characters and for his nonetheless mostly appreciative readers, Amis's talent—to take Allen's words exactly—is itself "uncomfortable": an attitude of mind which tends to be uneasy (at least up to the mid-1960s) with straight, unmodified statement, and to present with varying degrees of reservation not only the objects of his main characters' perceptions but those main characters themselves. It is this attitude—the result, perhaps, in the 1950s, of feeling part of a group of intellectuals intent on not being "taken in" by emotion—that produces the verbal texture, prickly with outward- and inward-facing irony, to which commentators have given the epithet "Amisian."

This characteristic style, with what David Lodge has called its "reflexive, self-scrutinizing element," and its air of questioning the validity of clichés of language and feeling, may well, as Lodge said in the early 1960s, "guarantee the sincerity of Amis's characters,"[4] but though it generates a great deal of wry verbal humor and suggests the uncertainty and unheroic quality of much human experience, it has simmered down in the last decade or so, and a passage in *That Uncertain Feeling* may indicate Amis's own discomfort with the ambivalence it involved. Walking by some tennis courts, his attention divided between a pretty girl in shorts and thoughts of Elizabeth Gruffydd-Williams (Ch. 5), John Lewis is accosted "with mistaken certainty" by "a large brown dog"; rebuffed, the dog bounds away in pursuit of a passing invalid-car. The location of "certainty" in a dog is ironical, to be sure; nevertheless Lewis comments ruefully as it disappears: "I envied him his committed air."

Virtually the earliest essay on Amis's work, John D. Hurrell's "Class and Conscience in John Braine and Kingsley Amis," published in 1958, pointed to the existence of a basic "sincerity" in Amis's novels, fleetingly visible under their shifting ironic surface: "Amis is essentially a serious writer . . . yet he is afraid of his own sincerity and has adopted an attitude of detached sophistication." This seems to me, as an observation on the early fiction, to be essentially true; more recently, in 1971, Norman Macleod has searchingly characterized Amis's linguistic fun as "a way of being serious" by examining "the trickiness of language," as a way both of seeking and of avoiding definite statement, and as a method (used by Amis's characters if not necessarily endorsed by their author) of sliding away from full confrontation with an awkward fact or a demanding moral problem.[5]

Macleod's essay, though published so long after Hurrell's, deals only with Amis's first five novels, and in a revealing footnote he admits that "it would be very difficult indeed to integrate" into his study the sixth and "most recent" novel, *The Anti-Death League*. Given the fact that even the Amis criticism of the last decade has hardly begun to take into detailed account the novels written after *The Anti-Death League*, it may well be that in the public mind an image of Amis as a "funny" novelist (and perhaps, even now, as mainly the author of *Lucky Jim*) still persists, despite the seriousness that, since the early 1960s, has worked its way to the surface of his fiction and greatly increased its "committed air" of conscious involvement with "permanent tendencies of heart and mind." If Amis can ever be called a funny novelist, it is mostly in the sense mentioned by Macleod in his article—not "Funny Ha-Ha" but "Funny Peculiar"; and the fact that his humor, when not (as so often) autonomously verbal, resides less in incidents depicted than in the depiction of incident is strongly suggested by his 1970 postscript to an essay of 1959 describing a public panel appearance Amis made—along with Jack Kerouac—in New York: "I think I make this sort of thing sound more fun to do than it actually is, but then this probably applies to written descriptions of all activities whatever."[6]

Chronologically the center of Amis's fiction, *The Anti-Death League* is also its major turning-point: from a kind of comedy (or the verbal simulacrum of it) to seriousness manifested in sobriety of language as well as in the virtual extinction of already diminishing comic incident. So unexpected was this shift of tone that, as Amis pointed out in the *Paris Review* in 1975, one puzzled critic visited him to ask, "Was I serious? Or was it all an elaborate farce or irony, couched in the form of some supposedly serious story?"[7] Hindsight—the fact, that, since *The Anti-Death League*, Amis has largely continued in recognizably serious vein—may make this puzzlement seem a ludicrous failure to respond to the obvious; but it was not entirely the critic's fault. Part of the fault lay with Amis himself: expectations set up by his early novels (which, admittedly, Amis was free at any time to frustrate) were likely to have been reinforced by more polemical nonfictional statements, such as his debunking early essays on Keats, Jane Austen, and D. H. Lawrence and remarks he made four years after publishing *Lucky Jim:*

The welfare democracy . . . is a satirical arena far vaster and richer than the stratified democracy which is now yielding place to it. . . . Until the new society is simplified and stabilized, which may not be for decades, we are in for what I have called a golden age of satire.[8]

This would appear, on the face of it, a long-term commitment to contribute to the satirical "golden age" oneself; but despite elements in Amis's novels which one cannot avoid calling satirical—laughter, amiable or sour, directed at the social detail of behavior, speech-habits and cultural fashions—Amis himself has more recently denied that he is a satirist or that, indeed, he "is making any kind of statement about 'society'": rather, his object as a novelist "is to portray human nature as it always has been, the permanent human passions of love, sorrow, ambition, fear, anger, frustration, joy and the rest."[9] The declaration, perhaps, reflects a feeling that the label "satirist" is too limiting, an excuse for the critic to set aside an author's serious intentions while praising his skill as an entertainer; such a critical attitude would not do justice to Amis's fiction, in whose view of human life the satirical is simply one element, but his own remark "Annoying people is part of one's life's work"[10] does little to deflect it.

Nevertheless, dissatisfaction with the limitations of the satirical stance itself (as distinct from the "satirist" label) appear in a poem published even earlier than Amis's remarks on a "golden age of satire," and could have alerted critics to a possible change of tone and direction later. The last lines of "Mightier than the Pen," which appeared in *A Case of Samples* in 1956, abandon an initial impulse to transfix with art's camera-eye an unpleasant individual:

> Cameras just click, and a click's not
> The sound of an effective shot;
> Fussing with flash and tripod's fun,
> But bang's the way to get things done.

The growing seriousness of Amis's fiction—"there's been an increase in the dim view which is taken of life, and the element of horseplay and high spirits decreases"[11]—may thus be viewed as the necessary compromise of a maturing author between the unavailability of murder and the practical limits of the satiric mode.

Up to and including *Take a Girl like You*, Amis's novels involve heroes who are broadly left-wing in sympathy, and the first two confront their protagonists with phenomena of right-wing culture—artistic snobberies in *Lucky Jim*, money and power in *That Uncertain Feeling*—against which they express their resentment in various ways. It was not altogether unreasonable, therefore, for journalists to think of Amis as an "Angry Young Man," and his remarks about an expanding "golden age of satire," read cursorily, might have given the impression that, if he were part of it, his sympathies would remain left-wing. Read more carefully, however, Amis's remarks promise nothing so simple: it is not the old-style "stratified democracy" (the old class system) that is to offer targets, but the new, fluid "welfare democracy" which is taking its place—a social melee in which shifting allegiances and an eventual change of sides are just as likely to occur. Hence, though the later "right-wing" positions taken up by Amis in various essays (hostility to pro-Communist myopia, hardening certainty that in university expansion "More will mean Worse"[12]) have caused even a well-disposed critic like Clive James to give him the expressive satirical nickname "Kingsley Kong,"[13] it would be incorrect to speak of a violent, unpredictable swing to "establishment" conservatism, and unfair to harbor the image of a middle-aged, successful Amis turning on his former self with the remark, "I'm all right, Jack" (or Jim). Rather there has been a gradual realization—evinced not only in a perhaps unwise taste for provocative public statement but through the subtler changes of stance of a succession of paraacademic and later nonacademic main characters—that a postwar world still solid enough to provoke a degree of iconoclasm had begun to crumble faster than its critics wished, into a gloom-engendering shapelessness that required not satire but last-minute efforts at consolidation.

While the crumbling itself, of course, is an external phenomenon, and the result partly of the likes and dislikes of generations junior to Amis's own, the perception of it is related to Amis's own gradual ageing: an objectively different world is observed by a subjectively changing novelist, whose set of priorities and emphases is itself undergoing the mutations of time. The universality of this inevitable process is suggested by the wry exaggeration which Amis puts in the mouth of Keith MacKelvie as he observes the old people in *Ending Up* (Ch. 29): "I suppose with luck we might get a couple of weeks between the last of them going and us being in their situation."

If one sets the beginning of Amis's career in fiction beside the (present) end of it, the gradual alteration his attitudes have undergone can be expressed as a striking contrast, in terms drawn from Evelyn Waugh, whose novels resemble Amis's not only by reason of their also being "serio-comedies"[14] whose seriousness increases, but because of a shared private joke: Amis's "L. S. Caton" motif recalls Waugh's recurrent references to C. R. M. F. Cruttwell, his history tutor at Oxford, who turns up as "General Cruttwell" the explorer in *Scoop* and as "Mr. Cruttwell," Brenda Last's bone-setter, in *A Handful of Dust*. Jim Dixon, out of place in provincial university society, has affinities with Hooper, the young subaltern with "a flat, Midland accent" who fits ill into the officers' mess of *Brideshead Revisited* and jars the romantic sensibilities of Captain Charles Ryder: "The history they taught him had had few battles in it but, instead, a profusion of detail about humane legislation and recent industrial change."[15] Jake Richardson, on the other hand (and, to a lesser extent, Douglas Yandell of *Girl, 20*), observes the world with an incomprehension, sad and apoplectic by turns, which recalls Evelyn Waugh himself, who noted in his diary at the age of sixty: "It was fun thirty-five years ago to travel far and in great discomfort to meet people whose entire conception of life and manner of expression were alien. Now one has only to leave one's gates."[16] There is, however, another resemblance which one should note, which provides a degree of continuity throughout Amis's protracted translation from the brave new world of Hooper to the disenchantment of his creator: that between Amis and Louis MacNeice, particularly the wry, witty, satirical, and serious MacNeice of *Autumn Journal* (1938), the decent yet detached observer, the "homme moyen sensuel" who combines an academic scepticism with a reaching toward belief.

At the beginning of this chapter, I quoted Walter Allen's view of Amis in 1954 and attempted to gloss the two epithets he used, "formidable" and "uncomfortable." It remains to stress the noun they qualified: "talent." Among the novelists of his own generation, who enjoyed their first fame in the 1950s—John Wain, John Braine, Alan Sillitoe, Iris Murdoch—Amis ranks very high. Indeed, it would be reasonable to call him a major novelist: altogether more subtle and versatile than Braine (who quite lacks his sensitivity of verbal texture); more interesting as a novelist than Wain, who is nevertheless as a man of letters equally wide-ranging; with more staying-power than Sillitoe (though Sillitoe's *Saturday Night and Sunday Morning* is not inferior as a single novel to *Lucky Jim*); lacking the philosophical dimension of Iris Murdoch, but counterbalancing this by a more idiosyncratic style and a greater vigor and immediacy of presentation. Amis's sharpness of eye and ear, his richness of comic invention (whether funny, wry, or bitter), his fertile diversity in the creation of minor characters, his ability to involve the reader in the consciousness of major characters whose predicaments brilliantly or darkly mirror his own—these virtues hardly need to be dwelt on and have, I hope, been adequately illustrated in my individual studies of novels and short stories. His fiction also possesses much tenderness and an increasing degree of compassion.

Nevertheless, though he is a major novelist, he is not yet a great one; he possesses a protean talent, but not genius. Greatness and genius are commodities admittedly rare among British novelists of the last thirty years; what they might be the name of William Golding, a generation older than Amis but a contemporary in terms of his literary appearance (1954), may approximately indicate. Unlike Golding, however, Amis has steered clear of literary experimentation, and indeed has remained throughout his career notably hostile to "tricks" and "foolery," aiming instead "to tell interesting, believable stories about understandable characters in a reasonably straightforward style."[17] Unlike Golding's, Amis's novels generally lack that enlarging resonance, that sense of the numinous which, though rather intimidating in Golding, could provide for novels set in the recognizable contemporary world that element of "expansion" desiderated by E. M. Forster, in *Aspects of the Novel*, for the greatest works of fiction. One of the most recent poems in Amis's *Collected Poems* is modeled on an epigram by Martial which Jake Richardson recites to his wife in a prose version in Chapter 3 of *Jake's Thing*:

> That time you heard the archbishop fart
>   You did quite right to say;
> And should the ploughboy turn up gold
>   The news would make our day;
> But when the ploughboy farts henceforth
>   Forget about it, eh?

This is entitled "Advice to a Story-Teller"; Amis has not invariably taken it.

David Lodge, in an essay originally published in 1963, with delicate acuity suggested the limitations inherent in Amis's choice of the contemporary, "realistic" mode of writing instead of the "modern," experimental one (which Lodge links with the work of James Joyce and Virginia Woolf):

His language, turned back at the metaphysical frontier, returns to sabotage the positivist, common-sense epistemology at the centre of his work, producing the sour, spoiling comedy which creates such dissonances in *Take a Girl Like You*.[18]

I take this to mean, essentially, that Amis can neither achieve an "expansion" from realism nor write as though he did not wish to achieve it. In 1969, Lodge looked again at Amis, taking into account what he had written since 1960, and saw in his interest in Ian Fleming (a writer of "romances") and in science fiction "a lust for fabulation" [as distinct from realistic writing] "repressed by his literary 'censor,' seeking outlet in certain licensed areas where traditional literary values are not expected to obtain." For Lodge, the writing of *Colonel Sun* "is surely a case of the realistic novelist taking a holiday from realism, finding a way to enjoy the forbidden fruit of romance without fully committing himself to the enterprise."[19]

Whether or not this is so in *Colonel Sun* (and Amis has certainly spoken recently of the possibility of experimenting not with style but with genre[20]), Amis's use of the "genre" novel from *The Anti-Death League* to *The Alteration* has certainly allowed him to suggest that the range of human experience is not confined to what occurs between birth and death, or to what is visible in the external, "realistic" world. Equally importantly, in my view, it has enabled him to speak emotionally, and with less need for protective irony (linguistically delightful as the expression of that irony can be in his novels). It is as if, within the conventions of genre, Amis has been released to be serious, most powerfully in *The Green Man, The Anti-Death League*, and *The Alteration*, all of them possessing in some degree a sense of the numinous. Elsewhere, too, without sacrificing the sharpness of his humor, Amis has been able to speak with a memorable seriousness and an impressive structural control: in *Lucky Jim, Girl, 20*, and *Ending Up*. To these six novels, which seem to me Amis's best, I would also add three short stories: "I Spy Strangers," austere, tolerant, and humorous; *Dear Illusion*, searching, poignant, and wry; and "All the Blood within

Me," whose moving penetration and economy of effect give it a special place in Amis's work. Together with the best of Amis's poems, these works of fiction assure him a very important place as "artist and entertainer" (his own modest view of himself[21]) among contemporary British writers.

What "keeps you going," Amis said in 1976, is "the notion that the next one may be a masterpiece."[22] If one feels Amis has not yet written a masterpiece, it is partly because his own achievement so far suggests the appropriateness of judging him by the highest literary standards. If he is able to develop further what he himself has called "my stunted spiritual faculties,"[23] add the result of that development to his unsparing and often witty observation of human life and behavior, and at the same time part with the half-commitment of genre (for surely the greatest writers can do without it?), he may well achieve the masterpiece of which he is capable.

Notes and References

Chapter One

1. See "I Remember, I Remember," *The Less Deceived* (Hull: The Marvell Press, 1955), p. 37.
2. Amis, interview with Melvyn Bragg, the *Listener*, February 20, 1975, p. 240.
3. "Bobby Bailey," *Collected Poems 1944–1979* (London: Hutchinson, 1979), p. 120.
4. Donald Davie, essay in *My Cambridge* (London: Robson Books, 1977), p. 94.
5. Philip Larkin, "Church Going," *The Less Deceived*, p. 27.
6. See his essay "In Slightly Different Form" (1969), reprinted in *What Became of Jane Austen? and Other Questions* (London: Cape, 1970), p. 108.
7. Ibid., pp. 192–98.
8. See "City Ways" (1958), ibid., p. 135.
9. Foreword to *New Maps of Hell* (New York: Harcourt, Brace, 1960), p. 7.
10. "City Ways," in *What Became of Jane Austen?*, p. 137.
11. A financially smaller award.
12. Amis, *Socialism and the Intellectuals* (London: Fabian Society, 1957), p. 1.
13. I quote the original poem as published in *Bright November* (London: Fortune Press, 1947). The version of it which appears in *Collected Poems* (1979) is verbally very different, replacing *inter alia* the original "scholarly" references to "Thorkelin's transcript B" and "Zupitza's reading."
14. Philip Larkin, Introduction to 1975 reissue of *Jill* (London: Fortune Press, 1946), p. 17.
15. Amis, in *The Poetry of War 1939–45*, ed. Ian Hamilton (London: Alan Ross, 1965), p. 157.
16. Amis, interview with Melvyn Bragg, The *Listener*, February 20, 1975, p. 240.
17. The story is printed in *My Enemy's Enemy* (London: Gollancz, 1962). Archer corresponds with a friend in Oxford who "was medically unfit for military service," and is written to "about issues of jazz records." Amis visited Oxford on leaves, usually to coincide with visits there by Philip Larkin, who graduated in 1943 and took a library post in Wellington, Shropshire.
18. John Wain, *Sprightly Running* (London: Macmillan, 1962), p. 188.

19. Amis, interview with Clive James, the *New Review* 1:4 (July 1974): 25. A detailed picture of Caton is given by Derek Stanford in *Inside the Forties* (London: Sidgwick & Jackson, 1977), pp. 30–33; also interesting are pages 7–8 of Philip Larkin's Introduction to the reissue of *The North Ship* (London: Faber, 1966).

20. Amis, "Lone Voices" (1960), in *What Became of Jane Austen?*, p. 165.

21. An Argentinian university occurs in *Lucky Jim:* L. S. Caton is appointed to a Chair at the University of Tucumán (Ch. 17). John Wain, in his second novel, *Living in the Present* (London: Secker & Warburg, 1955), refers to "some God-forsaken hole such as Tucumán" (Ch. 1)—presumably a private joke about Caton for Amis's benefit.

22. Professor James Kinsley, letter to the writer, April 22, 1976.

23. See "An Evening with Dylan Thomas" (1957) in *What Became of Jane Austen?*, pp. 57–62.

24. Amis, interview with Melvyn Bragg, p. 241.

25. The title was later changed to the far less forceful "A Bookshop Idyll."

26. Anon. review, The *Times Literary Supplement*, February 19, 1954.

27. Lionel Trilling, *E. M. Forster* (London: The Hogarth Press, 1944), p. 13.

28. W. Somerset Maugham, letter to *Sunday Times*, December 25, 1954.

29. Amis's attitude to "abroad," usually seen as hostile, is actually more ambivalent. Though he once wrote that he "went abroad for the first time—and then not voluntarily—in 1944," he elsewhere praised the army because it "got me away from home, sent me abroad for the first time." And before he obtained his post at Swansea, he "came second for a British Council post in Prague." So one cannot in full seriousness identify Garnet Bowen's attitudes with those of Amis himself.

30. Donald Davie, essay in *My Cambridge* (1977), p. 92.

31. I am indebted for this anecdote to Mrs. Olwen Hackett, formerly Lady Brogan, wife of the late Sir Denis Brogan, a senior Fellow of Peterhouse.

32. Amis's marriage to Hilary Bardwell was dissolved in that year.

33. Amis, "We mustn't let the rebels walk all over us," *TV Times*, August 16–22, 1975.

34. *New Poems 1977–78*, ed. Gavin Ewart (London: Hutchinson, 1978), p. 24; reprinted in Amis, *Collected Poems* (1979).

Chapter Two

1. For a splendidly dry paragraph on the situation, see C. Northcote Parkinson, *The Law and the Profits* (London: John Murray, 1960), p. 88.

2. See, for instance, "Why Lucky Jim Turned Right" (1967), and Amis's contributions (sometimes with Robert Conquest) to the *Black Papers* on education, in the 1970s.

3. Since 1957, Leicester University.

4. Amis, interview with Melvyn Bragg, p. 241.

5. The only other city in England with both a university (older than Leicester's) *and* a cathedral spire is Sheffield.

6. For a subtler indication of Amis's position, see the Postscript (1970) to the essay "No More Parades": "I went on keeping quiet for some time after that, wishing, for perhaps the hundredth time since arriving in Cambridge, that I were Jim Dixon." Dixon is surely invoked here as an uncouth rebel figure, rather than as the shy, put-upon young man he is for a large part of *Lucky Jim*.

7. Reference to this area is also worked into Chapter 24, when the bus-conductor congratulates Jim's catching of the moving bus with "Well run, wacker," the last word a specifically Merseyside (Liverpool) piece of slang.

8. Dale Salwak, "An Interview with Kingsley Amis," *Contemporary Literature*, Winter 1975, p. 10.

9. Philip Larkin, *The Whitsun Weddings* (London: Faber, 1964), p. 44.

10. Salwak, p. 5.

11. The collection of names is obviously comic, designed (with that of Michie) to cover the whole British Isles. More subtle is the spelling of "Welch," a more snooty version of "Welsh" (with its appropriate homophonic play on "welshing"), as is indicated by Robert Graves in *Goodbye to All That* (London: Cassell, 1929).

12. Salwak, p. 8.

13. Chapter 18: "A feeling of grief which was also a feeling of exasperation settled upon Dixon. He looked away over the fields beyond the nearby hedge to where a line of osiers marked the bed of a small stream." Chapter 24: ". . . he couldn't help feeling some sort of exhilaration especially at the brightness of the landscape under the sun. Beyond the lines of green-tiled semi-detached villas open fields were already appearing, and through some trees he could see a gleam of water." Both feelings are related to Dixon's thoughts about Christine.

14. David Lodge, "The Modern, the Contemporary, and the Importance of Being Amis," *Language of Fiction* (London: Routledge & Kegan Paul, 1966), p. 255.

15. *Lucky Jim's* theme repays comparison with that of Philip Larkin's poem "Reasons for Attendance," *The Less Deceived* (1955), p. 16.

16. The same trick is used in *Jake's Thing* in the description of the college porter's pronunciation of "I'll be bound" as "I'll be baned" (Ch. 10). The reason for Bertrand's "you sam," carefully explained by Amis, is credible: the actor Raymond Huntley, in an episode of the British TV serial "Upstairs, Downstairs," uttered quite naturally the word "evidentlam."

17. In terms of his army career, "Michie" recalls the poet Keith Douglas (born 1922), who left Oxford in 1940 and was a tank officer during the North African campaign. He was killed in Normandy in 1944.

18. *New Statesman*, January 30, 1954. William Cooper's novel is referred to in the *T.L.S.* review of *Lucky Jim*, February 12, 1954.

19. In his Introduction to the 1978 reprint (London: Secker & Warburg) of *Hurry on Down*, John Wain states that the first half of his novel was written between 1949 and mid-1951, the second half between the spring and summer of 1952. It was published in autumn 1953.

20. The first two lines of Amis's "old song"—"Oh Lucky Jim/How I envy him"—actually occur at the beginning of an earlier novel, Rosamond Lehmann's *A Note in Music* (London: Chatto & Windus, 1930).

21. Cf. Peter Firchow's interview with Amis in *The Writer's Place: Interviews on the Literary Situation in Contemporary Britain* (Minneapolis: University of Minnesota Press, 1974), p. 32.

22. Clive James, interview with Amis, p. 23. See also Amis, *Observer*, September 17, 1978, p. 35: "All I was trying to do [in *Lucky Jim*] is [*sic*] amuse people with the kind of stuff that had amused me in the work of people like Eric Linklater, P. G. Wodehouse and some of Evelyn Waugh."

23. Dixon's salary with Gore-Urquhart, £500 a year, is rather more than he would have earned as an Assistant Lecturer. The scale in 1954 was £450 to £550.

Chapter Three

1. Clive James interview, p. 22.

2. Reprinted in *What Became of Jane Austen?* (1970).

3. Chapter 8 indicates that, like Amis, Lewis is a devoted reader of *Astounding Science Fiction*, and one of the books on his shelves is *The Future of Swearing*, whose unindicated author is Robert Graves.

4. Clive James interview, p. 22.

5. As in the "Altar-wise by owl-light" sonnet sequence.

6. "Crew junction" is a pun on "Crewe Junction," a famous English railway station, and "sleepers" are the wooden ties under railway lines.

7. In Chapter 15 mention is made of Keidrych Rhys (editor of the journal *Wales*) by his real name; "Arwel Jenkins" recalls Arwel Hughes the Welsh conductor; and "Stan Johns," the Welsh composer, sounds like Dan Jones, the composer and boyhood friend of Dylan Thomas. All these references suggest that Amis is commentating here, rather than John Lewis.

8. In his interview with Dale Salwak Amis said that he didn't realize when writing the novel that Lewis was afraid of Elizabeth and "wanted out," so that his turning down the job was only the result of "half-scruples." It is, however, clear from Chapter 17 that Lewis does realize his mixed motives.

9. Since "Fforestfawr" is the name for the hill area north of Ystradgynlais, a small mining town at the head of the Swansea valley, it may be this town Amis has in mind; it was the locale of the Welsh National Eisteddfod which he visited, and which he describes in "Where Tawe Flows" (1954).

10. Salwak interview, p. 6.

11. Philip Larkin, *High Windows* (London: Faber, 1974), p. 34.

12. Salwak interview, p. 9.

13. Clive James interview, p. 23.

14. Salwak interview, p. 9.

15. Jenny's use of the idiom "wack" in her attack on Patrick (Ch. 13) suggests Liverpool, as does her trip to Southport Zoo. But other references—to Whitley Bay and Redcar (on the northeast coast of England)—may indicate that her home is in Yorkshire.

16. This quotation clearly anticipates the atmosphere of *The Riverside Villas Murder* (London: Cape, 1973).

17. The idea of "making love to someone you've drugged or intoxicated" is mentioned, reprehendingly, in Aldous Huxley's *Crome Yellow* (Ch. 29).

18. Like Beatrice, who is alluded to by the novel's epigraph (which refers to *Much Ado about Nothing*, Act II, Sc. I), Jenny will escape the fate—which perhaps her virginity-complex deserves—of "leading apes into Hell," the traditional fate of old maids. (Perhaps, however, Amis feels that Jenny does lead "apes"—the men who pursue her—into hell!)

19. Interview with Melvyn Bragg, p. 241.

Chapter Four

1. Philip Larkin, interviewed by Ian Hamilton, *London Magazine*, November 1964.

2. Amis, personal note prefixed to his poems in *Poets of the 1950's*, ed. D. J. Enright (Tokyo: Kenkyusha, 1955), p. 17.

3. Salwak interview, p. 7.

4. Further Joycean elements occur in Chapter 11 (Bowen's "generous tears" recall those of Gabriel in "The Dead") and in Chapter 10 (the reference to Bowen's photographs is in the style of the penultimate section of *Ulysses*).

5. Amis, *Socialism and the Intellectuals* (1957), p. 11.

6. An obvious reference to F. R. Leavis's admiration for Henry James. It is interesting to note that one of Strether's quaint "period" usages, "the public print" (for newspapers and journals), is repeated by Amis himself, in his own person, in the 1970 postscript to his essay "Kipling Good" (1962) (*What Became of Jane Austen?*, p. 177).

7. "Then Come Cuss Me," collected in Michael Frayn, *On the Outskirts* (London: Collins, 1964). The piece had previously appeared in the *Observer*. "Only resent" alludes to the epigraph of E. M. Forster's *Howards End:* "Only connect."

8. Salwak interview, p. 5. (It was published in 1975 but took place in 1973.)

9. James interview, p. 24. Amis added the rider: "until we get to Bernard Bastable" [of *Ending Up*].

10. The slang meaning of "roger" (to copulate with) expresses this.

11. Some of Amis's experiences in America, including having his script stolen *after* a lecture "at a well-known university in Philadelphia," are described in "Who Needs No Introduction" (1959), reprinted in *What Became of Jane Austen?*, pp. 152–57.

12. James interview, p. 25.

13. See "A New James Bond" (1968), reprinted in *What Became of Jane Austen?*, pp. 65–77.

14. The phrase is also used to convey the angry selfishness of the rich in Section Three, when Lady Baldock demands her champagne.

15. See *Lucky Jim's Politics* (London: Conservative Political Centre, 1968), p. 9.

16. In the Salwak interview (p. 11), Amis claims that the comic aspect of sex "is the only one one can hope to put into fiction." The statement does less than justice to his success in *I Want It Now* and in other novels.

Chapter Five

1. Amis, "A New James Bond," *What Became of Jane Austen?*, p. 70.

2. James interview, p. 25.

3. Amis's phrase in the Salwak interview, p. 16.

4. Amis, "Kipling Good," *What Became of Jane Austen?*, p. 174.

5. It is perhaps significant that a reference to "Eliot's notion of the objective correlative" is put in the mouth of Dr. Best, whom Amis in the Salwak interview (p. 7) calls a "completely bad" character.

6. In the James interview (p. 25), Amis states that "the fact that L. S. Caton finally gets bumped off in [*The Anti-Death League*] is a signal that it's to be taken seriously."

7. The geographical location of the novel is difficult to pin down, but at various points sufficiently precise detail is given to suggest firsthand experience. Amis may have in mind the area around Catterick at which he trained as a Signals Officer (it has a mixture of lushness and bleakness, and a number of Abbey ruins); alternatively he may be thinking of Charnwood Forest near Loughborough, which has abbeys, unusual rock formations, and (certainly in the 1950s) a Royal Signals camp.

8. The qualities of chivalry and bitterness, both present in *The Anti-Death League*, make me wonder whether Amis had in mind when choosing his title the British film of the 1950s *The League of Gentlemen*, which is a poignant presentation of military comradeship functioning (nefariously) in a postwar context.

9. An imaginary contemporary of the real Jonathan Battishill (1738–

1801). Amis's liking for Ayscue is conveyed by his being given Amis's own admiration for the music of C. P. E. (as opposed to J. S.) Bach.

10. Philip Larkin, *The Whitsun Weddings* (1964), p. 11.

11. James interview, p. 25.

12. This is Amis's term for Underhill (Salwak interview, p. 15).

13. Ibid., p. 16.

14. One, Brian W. Alldiss, is a writer of science fiction. Another, John Dankworth, is a jazz composer and saxophonist.

15. On the real road between these two places lies a small hamlet called Green End. Amis's choice of locale—no doubt familiar from his two years at Cambridge (1961–63)—may be a private gesture of respect toward George Orwell, who for some years after 1936 ran the village store at Wallington, three miles from Sandon. The *date* 1984 is mentioned in passing in Part 2.

16. See Elizabeth Jane Howard on Amis in *Vogue*, June 1978, p. 160.

17. Salwak interview, p. 15.

18. The dubious modern churchmanship displayed by Sonnenschein—a variant of Father Colgate in *One Fat Englishman*—is perhaps Amis's reaction to the social theology of bishops like Mervyn Stockwood (formerly of Southwark) and John Robinson (formerly of Woolwich). Sonnenschein "no doubt . . . would soon be off to some more spiritually challenging parish in London."

19. In "Casting the Runes," Karswell's last stop on his train to Dover is at Croydon West, three stations before Norbury—a fact that might well have captured Amis's imagination as a young reader.

20. "Casting the Runes," *The Collected Ghost Stories of M. R. James* (London: Edward Arnold, 1931), 1964 edn., pp. 241–42.

21. Salwak interview, p. 15.

Chapter Six

1. See his remarks (pp. 29–30) in the Firchow interview (1974).

2. Philip Larkin, "Home Is So Sad," *The Whitsun Weddings* (1964), p. 17.

3. An invitation to outwit the author is extended on p. 6 of the Panther edition of the novel (1974).

4. George Orwell, "Decline of the English Murder" (1946). For Orwell, the heyday of the morally satisfying murder was 1850 to 1925.

5. James was Provost of Eton College. Peter Furneaux does not yet, apparently, know about his ghost stories.

6. See his essay on it, "Pater and Old Chap" (1957), reprinted in *What Became of Jane Austen?*, pp. 37–41.

7. The names Amis and Furneaux both have an Old French origin (though Colonel Manton calls Furneaux a Channel Islands, not a Normandy,

name). Curiously enough, of the very few examples of the name "Furneaux" which occur in the London Telephone Directory (1962 edn.), two belong to firms—one a Chartered Accountants—in the nearest large shopping street to Norbury, Streatham High Road.

8. Peter's relatives, on his father's side, come visiting from Denmark Hill (where Amis's parents met), and Peter takes regular holidays at East Runton in Norfolk (Amis's grandfather came from Norfolk). See "A Memoir of My Father," reprinted in *What Became of Jane Austen?*, pp. 192–200.

9. Amis's own description of him (James interview, p. 23).

10. The first two appeared in *Old Lights for New Chancels* (London: John Murray, 1940); the third in *New Bats in Old Belfries (London: John Murray, 1945)*.

11. See James interview, p. 28.

12. In *New Maps of Hell* (1960), Amis speaks of a not very good SF play by himself, unsuccessfully broadcast by the BBC's Third Programme (p. 86).

13. James interview, p. 28.

14. Warwick Deeping's *Sorrell and Son* (London: Cassell, 1925) may also have made a contribution here. On p. 49 Thomas Roland, speaking of ill-attended services at "Staunton" cathedral, describes "organ notes quaking, and a boy's voice soaring up to the grey roof like a bird."

15. The contemporary Italian Communist leader.

16. The "Prefect of Devotions" who announces Lights Out bears a distinct resemblance to the Prefect of Studies at Clongowes Wood College in Joyce's *A Portrait of the Artist as a Young Man*.

17. Well known for his singing of "Hear My Prayer" and "O for the wings of a dove."

18. All three, as well as being politically active, the first two in the Labour party, the third (Corin/Vanessa Redgrave) in the Workers' Revolutionary party, are extreme left-wing zealots. As with Berlinguer, Amis's point is presumably that the Church would employ such people if *it* were the government. Calling Anthony Wedgwood-Benn (or rather, Tony Benn, the matey style he now prefers) by his repudiated family title of Lord Stansgate is a further twist of right-wing sarcasm on Amis's part. For the use of these real names cf. Amis's hope expressed in *New Maps of Hell* (1960) that science fiction would move on "from satirising politicians and corporations to really spiteful attacks on politician A and corporation B" (pp. 86–87).

19. Socialist Prime Minister—from Yorkshire—at the time the book was written.

20. One of the resultant outbreaks of plague (Ch. 2) occurs in East Runton. See note 8.

21. John Wyndham's SF novel, set in a future world dominated by a kind of repressive Fundamentalism, was published in 1955 (London: Michael Joseph). Chapter 12 describes the escape of the clairvoyant children by night, on two "great-horses."

22. I am indebted for this medical corroboration of Amis's device to my friend Dr. Claire Neville-Smith, Medical Officer of Health for Schools, Newfoundland and Labrador.

23. Philip Larkin, "Dockery and Son," *The Whitsun Weddings* (1964), p. 38.

24. Cf. Philip Larkin, "Ignorance" (ibid., p. 39): we "spend all our life on imprecisions,/That when we start to die/Have no idea why."

Chapter Seven

1. Philip Larkin, "Dockery and Son," *The Whitsun Weddings* (1964), p. 38.

2. Decuman, one of Hubert's friends in *The Alteration*, comes from Barnet, and the monk who goes "to the pulley" is from "a monastery, at a place called Hadley" (Ch. 3). The full name of Hadley is, in fact, Monken Hadley.

3. James interview, p. 27.

4. See Amis's remarks in the Firchow interview (1974): "I think I'd do away with the Arts Council. I don't like the notion of the state handing out bursaries and awards to favoured writers" (p. 18).

5. It is an interesting coincidence, perhaps, that Amis's collection of essays, *What Became of Jane Austen?*, published the year before *Girl, 20*, is dedicated to Anthony Powell and his wife.

6. One of the events of the "night of the favour" (Ch. 3) is a graphically described wrestling-match. Amis had taken Elizabeth Jane Howard to one on their honeymoon (in Brighton) in 1965 (*Woman's Journal*, June 1976, p. 20).

7. The final phrase recalls Patrick Standish's full realization of his caddishness in "raping" Jenny Bunn.

8. Some light is shed on Douglas's possible "problem" here by an uncollected poem by Philip Larkin, "Love" (*Critical Quarterly* 8:2 [Summer 1966]: 173).

9. The meeting with Mr. Copes provides the nearest thing in the novel to a moral touchstone, and suggests Douglas as a person who exists halfway between a morality based on religious belief and a total lack of morality: he can neither propose to Vivienne nor leave her alone, while retaining a conventional shyness which prevents him from admitting to her father that he sleeps with her. Mr. Copes is presented without irony, and likes science fiction (a usual sign of authorial approval in Amis). Curiously, the otherwise "immoral" Roy and Sylvia intend to marry, though this if anything increases the destructiveness of their relationship to others.

10. James interview, p. 21.

11. The location of *Ending Up* was perhaps suggested to Amis by his time at Cambridge (Newmarket is twelve miles to the east); it may be significant that, some six miles southeast of Newmarket (the likeliest direction), there are tiny hamlets called Upend and Upend Green. Before England's currency

turned metric (2½ d. = the present 1 p.), a "tuppence-hapenny" stamp used frequently to be referred to by people of the Bastables' generation as a "tuppenny-hapenny" stamp.

12. The opening sentence of L. P. Hartley's *The Go-Between* (London: Hamish Hamilton, 1953).

13. Marigold's late husband is described as a glass merchant, the trade followed by Amis's paternal grandfather; Marigold's fussy smartness and social pretension are underscored by the mention of her former address, Beauchamp Place in London, off the Brompton Road near Harrods store.

14. At the fictitious "University of Northampton"—the alma mater of Chris Vandervane in *Girl, 20*.

15. Amis's own anticommunism is reflected by George Zeyer's views; the defence of Mihailović (always depicted as having collaborated with the Germans in Yugoslavia) is a kind of outrageous extension of this into earlier history.

16. Philip Larkin's poem "The Old Fools" (*High Windows*, 1974, pp. 19–20) also states this question, and provides in effect a commentary on *Ending Up*.

17. There may be a private joke involved in Amis's use of this name. The English poet Alan Brownjohn is the author of the British Council *Writers and Their Work* pamphlet on Philip Larkin (1975).

18. A TV panel game Amis has appeared on, which features what its compère, Robert Robinson, has referred to as "discontinued lines from the *O.E.D.*"

19. Firchow interview, p. 32.

20. The two novels relate to each other in another way, as Clive James pointed out in his review of *Jake's Thing* (*Observer*, September 17, 1978): "In Jake Richardson, Patrick Standish . . . reaches the end of the line."

21. A rank of greater rarity and moment at Oxford and Cambridge than at other United Kingdom universities.

22. Even the large number of chapters is a return to Amis's earlier practice, modified by their being given titles, as in *Girl, 20*.

23. As if to point up the overtones of *Lucky Jim* in Kelly's attempted suicide, Chapter 24 contains a phrase reminiscent of the passage where Jim hears the voice of Barclay, the Professor of Music. Jake notices in the conference room "what looked like, and proved indeed to be, a TV set."

24. Interview with Auberon Waugh, *Sunday Telegraph*, September 17, 1978, p. 36.

25. Interview with Pearson Phillips, *Observer*, September 17, 1978, p. 35. In 1976 Amis was made an honorary fellow of his old Oxford College, St. John's, so may have had some experience of the women's admission issue at first hand. How far his description of Oxford dons is *à clef* is debatable, but the reference (Chs. 10 and 20) to "the historian of drama who put on plays full of naked junior members of the university torturing one another" is applicable—if a slight exaggeration—to the poet and English don Francis

Warner: a scene from such a play by him was included in a TV documentary about Oxford a few years ago.

26. Transparent disguises for *Penthouse* and *Mayfair; Agora* is, equally clearly, *Forum*.

27. One of their models, Rosa Domaille, was an old favorite of Amis himself. (See James interview, p. 24. Rosa Domaille was the basis for Joan in *Take a Girl like You*.) The two other models Jake remembers, Anne Austin and June Palmer, are also genuine.

28. *Collected Poems* (1979), p. 122.

29. Cf. "Shitty" (note 28 above): "Each of them a sight more lovely/Than the screens around your bed."

Chapter Eight

1. Salwak interview, p. 16.

2. Ibid.

3. Philip Toynbee, "Novelist on Parnassus," *Observer*, April 8, 1979.

4. Firchow interview, pp. 17–18.

5. First published in 1949, and reprinted in *A Case of Samples* (London: Gollancz, 1956).

6. Amis's italics.

7. James interview, p. 25.

8. "Lament," *Bright November* (1947), p. 5.

9. James interview, p. 27.

10. The presence of Auden in Amis's work in the 1950s is not confined to his poetry. Chapter 1 of *Lucky Jim* has a phrase—"steering it between a collapse into helpless fatigue and a tautening with anarchic fury"—that sounds like a garbled memory of the last two lines of Auden's poem "Consider this and in our time": "To disintegrate on an instant in the explosion of mania/Or lapse for ever into a classic fatigue." At the end of Ch. 15 of *I Like It Here*, Garnet Bowen quotes Auden directly: "Again the driver pulls on his gloves . . . and in a blinding snowstorm, pity about that, starts upon his deadly journey, and again the writer runs howling to his art, well anyway" (cf. Auden, "Journey to Iceland").

11. "The Shield of Irony," *Times Literary Supplement*, April 2, 1954.

12. Robert Conquest, Introduction to *New Lines* (London: Macmillan, 1956), p. xv.

13. D. J. Enright was teaching in Japan at the time, at Kōnan University in Kobe. Kenkyusha, his Japanese publishers, brought out many books in English, on topics of interest to Japanese students of English literature, including the earliest version (1950) of G. S. Fraser's *The Modern Writer and His World*.

14. *Poets of the 1950's* (Tokyo: Kenkyusha, 1955), pp. 17–18.

15. The original title, after Stella Gibbons's phrase in *Cold Comfort Farm:* "something nasty in the woodshed."

16. G. S. Fraser, *The Modern Writer and His World* (Harmondsworth: Pelican Edn., 1964), p. 348: "a situation is clearly presented, a judgement is made upon it, the reader is invited to agree with the writer's judgement."

17. It is a reference to Sheila Torkington and the *"business"* spoken of to Patrick Standish by her father: "it had most probably involved advanced sexual play with some drunk in a shop-front opposite a well-attended bus stop."

18. Donald Davie, *Thomas Hardy and British Poetry* (London: Routledge & Kegan Paul, 1972), p. 100.

19. Amis did this himself while at Swansea. "Maunders," the title of his poem, is a joke-version of Mumbles, a beach resort near Swansea. (See "Age-Old Ceremony at Mumbles," 1956, reprinted in *What Became of Jane Austen?*, pp. 147–51.)

20. A seaside town between Swansea and Cardiff. (A London couple, bound on the same errand, would have gone to Brighton.)

21. The colloquial phrase refers punningly to the cross.

22. Amis, in his author's note, says twenty, presumably counting the three "Shorts" and the two "Impromptus" as single poems.

23. The title seems intended to refer to the book *My Oxford* (London: Robson Books, 1977), a collection of reminiscences by undergraduates of various periods who later became well known; one of them was Amis's son Martin, now a novelist.

24. John Betjeman, "Dorset," *Collected Poems*, pp. 38–39.

25. Thomas Hardy, "Friends Beyond," *Collected Poems* (London: Macmillan), pp. 52–54.

Chapter Nine

1. Salwak interview, p. 13.

2. Amis, prefatory note to *Dear Illusion* (London: Covent Garden Press, 1972).

3. Other characters named Dalessio crop up in *That Uncertain Feeling* (Ch. 6), and Frank Gioberti in "All the Blood within Me" is also part Italian. The motif is sufficiently unusual in itself and widespread in Amis's work to suggest a possible origin in people Amis knew.

4. Amis has stated: "I was the unfortunate Lieutenant Archer who was given a bad time by his Company Commander." (Interview, *Paris Review* XVI [Winter 1975]: 43.)

5. The middle-class suburb of Purley lies only a few miles to the south of Amis's Norbury.

6. Balham is some three miles north of Norbury.

7. James interview, p. 28.

8. Ibid.

9. Amis, interview in the *Sunday Times* (Colour Supplement), February 3, 1974, p. 64.

10. The title of his poem "Drizzle and Thrush," and his small stature, call up a passing image of Hardy.

Chapter Ten

1. *New Statesman and Nation*, January 30, 1954.
2. *The Situation of the Novel* (Harmondsworth: Pelican Edition, 1972), pp. 192, 194–95.
3. Ibid., p. 199.
4. *Language of Fiction* (1966), p. 259.
5. Norman Macleod, "*This familiar regressive series:* Aspects of Style in the Novels of Kingsley Amis," in *Edinburgh Studies in English and Scots* (London: Longman, 1971), pp. 121–43.
6. "Who Needs No Introduction" (1959), reprinted in *What Became of Jane Austen?* (1970), p. 156.
7. "The Art of Fiction LIX—Kingsley Amis," *Paris Review* XVI (Winter 1975): 56.
8. *New York Times Book Review*, July 7, 1957, p. 1.
9. Amis on himself, in *Contemporary Novelists* (London: St. James Press, 2nd edition, 1976), p. 44.
10. Amis, interview with Melvyn Bragg (1975), p. 241.
11. Salwak interview, p. 7.
12. "Lone Voices" (1960), reprinted in *What Became of Jane Austen?*, p. 161. Amis's contributions to the *Black Papers* on education express more fancifully, but with no reduction of force, the same views ("élitist" to some, mere common-sense to others).
13. Clive James, *The Improved Version of Peregrine Prykke's Pilgrimage through the London Literary World* (London: Cape, 1976), pp. 61–65.
14. Amis describes his own novels by this term in *Contemporary Novelists* (1976), p. 44.
15. Evelyn Waugh, *Brideshead Revisited* (London: Chapman and Hall, 1945), Prologue.
16. *The Diaries of Evelyn Waugh*, ed. Michael Davie (London: Weidenfeld & Nicolson, 1976), p. 791.
17. Amis, *Contemporary Novelists* (1976), p. 44.
18. David Lodge, *Language of Fiction* (1966), p. 260.
19. "The Novelist at the Crossroads" (1969), reprinted in David Lodge, *The Novelist at the Crossroads, and other essays on fiction and criticism* (London: Routledge & Kegan Paul, 1971), p. 20.
20. *Paris Review* interview (1975), p. 47.
21. Salwak interview, p. 18.
22. Amis, interviewed in *Woman's Journal*, June 1976, p. 21.
23. *Observer* Magazine, April 1, 1979, p. 61.

Selected Bibliography

PRIMARY SOURCES

1. NOVELS

Lucky Jim. London: Gollancz, 1954. New York: Doubleday, 1954.
That Uncertain Feeling. London: Gollancz, 1955. New York: Harcourt Brace, 1956.
I Like It Here. London: Gollancz, 1958. New York: Harcourt Brace, 1958.
Take a Girl like You. London: Gollancz, 1960. New York: Harcourt Brace, 1961.
One Fat Englishman. London: Gollancz, 1963. New York: Harcourt Brace, 1964.
The Egyptologists. (with Robert Conquest). London: Cape, 1965. New York: Random House, 1966.
The Anti-Death League. London: Gollancz, 1966. New York: Harcourt Brace, 1966.
Colonel Sun (as Robert Markham). London: Cape, 1968. New York: Harper, 1968.
I Want It Now. London: Cape, 1968. New York: Harcourt Brace, 1969.
The Green Man. London: Cape, 1969. New York: Harcourt Brace, 1970.
Girl, 20. London: Cape, 1971. New York: Harcourt Brace, 1972.
The Riverside Villas Murder. London: Cape, 1973. New York: Harcourt Brace, 1973.
Ending Up. London: Cape, 1973. New York: Harcourt Brace, 1974.
The Alteration. London: Cape, 1976. New York: The Viking Press, 1977.
Jake's Thing. London: Hutchinson, 1978. New York: The Viking Press, 1979.

2. SHORT STORIES

My Enemy's Enemy. London: Gollancz, 1962. New York: Harcourt Brace, 1963.
Dear Illusion. London: Covent Garden Press, 1972.
"The House on the Headland." *The Times*, November 24,. 1979.

166

3. POETRY

Bright November. London: The Fortune Press, 1947.
A Frame of Mind. Reading: University of Reading School of Art, 1953.
[Poems]. Eynsham: The Fantasy Press, 1954 (Fantasy Press Pamphlet No. 22).
A Case of Samples (Poems 1945–1956). London: Gollancz, 1956. New York: Harcourt Brace, 1957.
The Evans Country. Oxford: The Fantasy Press, 1962.
Penguin Modern Poets 2. Harmondsworth: Penguin Books, 1962. (Contains poems by Amis, Dom Moraes, and Peter Porter.)
A Look Round the Estate (Poems 1957–1967). London: Cape, 1967. New York: Harcourt Brace, 1968.
Collected Poems 1944–1979. London: Hutchinson, 1979. New York: The Viking Press, 1980.

4. CRITICISM

What Became of Jane Austen? and Other Questions. London: Cape, 1970.
Selected Stories of G. K. Chesterton. London: Faber, 1972.
Tennyson (selected and introduced by Kingsley Amis). Harmondsworth: Penguin Books, 1973.
"'Four Fluent Fellows': An Essay on Chesterton's Fiction." *Encounter*, October 1973, pp. 94–100.
Rudyard Kipling and His World. London: Thames & Hudson, 1975.
The New Oxford Book of Light Verse (ed. Kingsley Amis). London: Oxford University Press, 1978.

5. MISCELLANEOUS

Oxford Poetry 1949 (ed. Kingsley Amis and James Michie). Oxford: Basil Blackwell, 1949.
Socialism and the Intellectuals. London: Fabian Society, 1957. (Fabian Tract 304).
New Maps of Hell: A Survey of Science Fiction. London: Gollancz, 1961. New York: Harcourt Brace, 1960.
Spectrum. A Science Fiction Anthology (ed. Amis and Robert Conquest). London: Gollancz, 1961.
Spectrum II, III & IV (ed. Amis and Conquest). London: Gollancz, 1962, 1963, 1965.
The James Bond Dossier. London: Cape, 1965.
Lucky Jim's Politics. London: Conservative Political Centre, 1968.
On Drink. London: Cape, 1972. New York: Harcourt Brace, 1973.

Harold's Years (ed. Kingsley Amis). London: Quartet Books, 1977.
The Faber Popular Reciter (ed. Kingsley Amis). London: Faber, 1978.

SECONDARY SOURCES

1. CHECKLISTS

GOHN, JACK B. *Kingsley Amis: A Checklist.* Kent, Ohio: Kent State University Press, 1976.
RABINOVITZ, RUBIN. Bibliography of works by and about Kingsley Amis, in *The Reaction against Experiment in the English Novel, 1950–1960.* New York and London: Columbia University Press, 1967, pp. 174–84.
SALWAK, DALE. *Kingsley Amis.* Boston: G. K. Hall and Co., 1978.
VANN, J. DONN, and TANNER, J. T. F. "Kingsley Amis: A Checklist of Recent Criticism." *Bulletin of Bibliography* 26:4 (October-December 1969): pp. 105, 111, 115–17.

2. INTERVIEWS WITH AMIS

BARBER, MICHAEL. "The Art of Fiction—LIX: Kingsley Amis." *Paris Review* XVI (Winter 1975): 39–72.
BRAGG, MELVYN. "Kingsley Amis Looks Back." *The Listener*, February 20, 1975, pp. 240–41.
FIRCHOW, PETER. "Kingsley Amis," in *The Writer's Place: Interviews on the Literary Situation in Contemporary Britain.* Minneapolis: University of Minnesota Press, 1974, pp. 15–38.
JAMES, CLIVE. "Kingsley Amis." *The New Review* 1:4 (July 1974): 21–28.
SALWAK, DALE. "An Interview with Kingsley Amis." *Contemporary Literature* 16:1 (Winter 1975): 1–18.
WAUGH, AUBERON. "Amis: A Singular Man." *Sunday Telegraph Magazine*, September 17, 1978, pp. 33–36.
WOODWARD, IAN. "Kingsley Amis and Elizabeth Jane Howard: A Lovely Couple." *Woman's Journal*, June 1976, pp. 19–21.

3. ARTICLES ON AMIS (INCLUDING CHAPTERS IN BOOKS)

BERGONZI, BERNARD. Section 2 of Ch. 6, "Between Nostalgia and Nightmare," in *The Situation of the Novel.* London: Macmillan, 1970 (Pelican Books, 1972, pp. 189–204). Perceptive treatment of Amis's novels up to *The Anti-Death League*, with some interesting comments on Amis's "deft" and "glum" poems.

CAPLAN, RALPH. "Kingsley Amis," in *Contemporary British Novelists*, ed. Charles Shapiro. Carbondale: Southern Illinois University Press, 1965, pp. 3–15. Concentrates on Amis as a "funny" writer and as an enemy of affectation.

CONQUEST, ROBERT. "Christian Symbolism in 'Lucky Jim.'" *Critical Quarterly* VII:1 (Spring 1965): 87–92. A spoof article, reducing to absurdity the scholarly temptation to overingenuity in textual analysis. (It was taken seriously by many readers, as an editorial in the Autumn 1965 issue, p. 203, points out with astonishment!)

DAVIE, DONALD. "Lucky Jim and the Hobbits." Ch. 4 of *Thomas Hardy and British Poetry*. London and New York: Oxford University Press, 1972, pp. 83–104. A treatment of Amis's poetry which blends ideological and aesthetic considerations; hostile to *A Look Round the Estate*, more favorable to *A Case of Samples*.

FALLIS, RICHARD. "*Lucky Jim* and Academic Wishful Thinking." *Studies in the Novel* IX:1 (Spring 1977): 65–72. Sees *Lucky Jim*'s appeal as greater than that of Amis's other novels; Jim Dixon is "a fantasized version of our unrealized selves," and the novel is "a version of heroic fantasy cast into superficially realistic situations."

GINDIN, JAMES. "Kingsley Amis's Funny Novels." Ch. 3 of *Postwar British Fiction: New Accents and Attitudes*. Berkeley: University of California Press, 1962, pp. 34–50. Lively treatment of Amis's first four novels, seeing their unity as consisting in a "comic acceptance of the contemporary scene." *That Uncertain Feeling* is Amis's "best, and least consoling, novel."

GREEN, MARTIN. "British Comedy and the British Sense of Humor: Shaw, Waugh and Amis." *Texas Quarterly* IV:3 (1961): 217–27. Whereas Waugh exemplifies an aristocratic humor, Amis, though not yet his equal, has begun "to create a sense of humor for the other half, the Lawrentian, relatively inarticulate half of Britain." His heroes are "average, normal, decent." Amis's humor is "more moral" than that of Shaw and Waugh, also "essentially embarrassed and resentful, or revengeful."

HOPKINS, ROBERT H. "The Satire of Kingsley Amis's *I Like It Here*." *Critique* VIII:3 (Spring-Summer 1966): 62–70. Cogently defends *I Like It Here* against the view that, for lack of an adequate plot, it fails as a novel. Rather it is an "aesthetic satire," "a novel of literary attack" on both F. R. Leavis's *The Great Tradition* and the "angry-young-man stereotype" critics had applied to Amis.

HOWARD, ELIZABETH JANE. "Kingsley Amis." *Vogue*, June 1978, pp. 158–60, 183. A personal view of Amis by his second wife.

HURRELL, JOHN D. "Class and Conscience in John Braine and Kingsley Amis." *Critique* II:1 (1958): 39–53. The 1950s crisis of the "young man without a distinctive class-allegiance" is treated by Braine as tragedy, by Amis as comedy (a harder task). Hurrell reads the texts of Amis's first three novels with great respect for detail, and is very sensible about their mixture of the comic and the serious.

HUTCHINGS, W. "Kingsley Amis's Counterfeit World." *Critical Quarterly* XIX:2 (Summer 1977): 71–77. A perceptive review article on *The Alteration.*

LODGE, DAVID. "The Modern, the Contemporary and the Importance of Being Amis." Ch. 7 of *Language of Fiction.* London: Routledge & Kegan Paul. New York: Columbia University Press, 1966, pp. 242–67. Excellent study of Amis's language effects in his first four novels, and of their relation to his position as a "post-modernist," traditional writer of fiction.

MACLEOD, NORMAN. "*This familiar regressive series:* Aspects of Style in the Novels of Kingsley Amis," in *Edinburgh Studies in English and Scots,* ed. Aitken, McIntosh, and Pálsson. London: Longman 1971, pp. 121–43. Very subtle, thorough, and excellently illustrated study of Amis's characteristic linguistic effects in his first five novels; these effects are related both to Amis's search for exactitude and his (or his heroes') avoidance of it.

MELLORS, JOHN. "A Piano-Tuner's Ear: The Novels of Kingsley Amis." *London Magazine* XIV (August-September 1974): pp. 102–106. A rather hasty look at the whole of Amis's fiction, emphasising its funniness and its sharp ear for affectations of behavior and of speech.

O'CONNOR, WILLIAM VAN. "Kingsley Amis: That Uncertain Feeling." Ch. 5 of *The New University Wits, and the End of Modernism.* Carbondale: Southern Illinois University Press, 1963, pp. 75–102. A sensible and shrewd overview of Amis's work up to *Take a Girl like You.* Amis is the "voice" of his generation, despite not particularly wanting to be; his novels are social documents, without his wanting to be thought of as a "social novelist."

PARKER, R. B. "Farce and Society: The Range of Kingsley Amis." *Wisconsin Studies in Contemporary Literature* II:3 (1961): 27–38. A shrewd commentary, provoked by *Take a Girl like You,* on the only apparent "realism" of Amis's view of people and events.

RABINOVITZ, RUBIN. Ch. 2 of *The Reaction against Experiment in the English Novel, 1950–1960.* New York and London: Columbia University Press, 1967, pp. 38–63. A well-documented study of Amis, placing him in the context of his contemporaries in England and the United States; in relation to the postwar reaction against modernism in the novel; and in relation to eighteenth-century writers like Fielding and Richardson. For Rabinovitz, Amis is far from being just an "Angry Young Man."

ROBERTS, G. O. "Love and Death in an English Novel: *The Anti-Death League* Investigated," in *A Festschrift for Edgar Ronald Seary,* Memorial University of Newfoundland, 1975, pp. 201–14. A crisp and comprehensive discussion of the themes and characters of *The Anti-Death League*.

STOVEL, BRUCE, "Traditional Comedy and the Comic Mask in Kingsley Amis's *Lucky Jim*." *English Studies in Canada* IV:1 (Spring 1978): 69–80. Relates *Lucky Jim* to the traditional devices and patterns of stage comedy and to *Tom Jones*. Places great emphasis on Jim's "faces" as the modern equivalent of comic masks; attempts to account for the *intensity* of the exhilaration and laughter provided by *Lucky Jim*.

VORHEES, RICHARD J. "Kingsley Amis: Three Hurrahs and a Reservation." *Queen's Quarterly* LXXIX (Spring 1972): 38–46. Discusses the decent morality of Amis's first three novels, and their essentially "good" heroes. Prefers the earlier novels to the later, and doubts the wisdom of Amis's spending time writing a novel like *Colonel Sun*. Amis "has perhaps dissipated his talents as well as developed them."

Index

Allen, Walter, 34, 144, 145, 149

Amis, Kingsley, childhood and youth, 13–14, 46; at university, 15–18; in the army, 16–17, 136; at University College, Swansea, 18–19, 38; early critical reception, 19–20, 118; visits to America, 21, 55, 58; at Cambridge, 21–22; second marriage and life in London, 22, 93, 132; children in work of, 77; death of father, 127

FICTION:

"All the Blood within Me," *138–41,* 143, 151, 152

Alteration, The, 77, *83–91,* 105, 151

Anti-Death League, The, 16, 59, *63–71,* 75, 77, 80, 86, 93, 116, 126, 133, 134, 140, 146, 151

Colonel Sun, 58, 63, 132, 151

"Court of Enquiry", 136

"Dear Illusion", *141–43,* 151

Ending Up, 99–105, 108, 148, 149, 151

Egyptologists, The, 132–33

Girl, 20, 92–99, 151

Green Man, The, 71–76, 77, 78, 92, 99, 151

"House on the Headland, The", 141

I Like It Here, 18, 19, 21, 44, *50–53,* 55, 58, 102, 106, 111, 133, 141

"Interesting Things", 134

"I Spy Strangers", 17, 135, *136–38,* 151

I Want It Now, 58–62, 63

Jake's Thing, 105–12, 133, 150

Legacy, The, 18

Lucky Jim, 16, 19, 20, 21, *22–36,* 37, 38, 39, 60, 67, 106, 107, 146, 147, 148, 150, 151

"Moral Fibre", 134–35

My Enemy's Enemy, 16, 64, *133–41*

"My Enemy's Enemy", 135, 136

One Fat Englishman, 18, *53–57,* 63

Riverside Villas Murder, The, 13, 77, *78–82,* 83, 105, 140

"Sacred Rhino of Uganda, The", 15

"Something Strange", 133–34

Take a Girl Like You, 42–48, 53, 63, 68, 99, 105, 121, 127, 148

That Uncertain Feeling, 21, 22, *37–42,* 43, 134, 145, 148

POETRY:

"Act of Kindness", 118

"Advice to a Story-Teller", 150

"After Goliath", 123, 126–27

"Aiming at a Million", 118

"Against Romanticism", 119, 121–22

"Belgian Winter", 117

"Beowulf", 16, 114

"Berkhamsted", 18, 117

"Bobby Bailey", 13, 81, 129, 140–41

Bright November, 16, 18, *114–18,* 129

Case of Samples, A, 118–23, 124, 147

"Chromatic Passing-Note, A", 124

Collected Poems, 113, *128–31*

"Crisis Song", 128

"Dream of Fair Women, A", 19, 122–23

"Drinking Song", 128

"Evans Country, The", 123, 124–25

"Farewell Blues", 131

Frame of Mind, A, 19, 20, 118

"For Elisabeth's Birthday", 115

"Huge Artifice, The", 124, 125–26

"In Memoriam W.R.A.", 127–28

"Larger Truth", 125

"Last War, The", 118

"Legends", 118

"Letter to Elisabeth", 115

Look Round the Estate, A, 123–28

"Masters", 114

"Mightier than the Pen", 147
"New Approach Needed", 124, 126
"Nicely", 128
"Nocturne", 121
"Nothing to Fear", 127
"Ode to Me", 128
"Prelude", 15
"Radar", 115
"Release", 17, 116
"Reunion, A", 17, 22, 129
"Shitty", 111, 128-29
"Something Nasty in the Bookshop"
  ("A Bookshop Idyll"), 19, 120
"Something was Moaning in a
  Corner", 119
"Song of Experience, A", 122-23
"Their Oxford", 129-31
"Value of Suffering, The", 118
"Where are You?", 116

MISCELLANEOUS:
Lucky Jim's Politics, 127
"Memoir of My Father, A", 14, 79
New Maps of Hell, 21
"No More Parades", 21
"On Christ's Nature", 63, 64, 75
Socialism and the Intellectuals, 27,
  52, 127
"Why Lucky Jim Turned Right", 93

Amis, Rosa, 14
Amis, Sally, 16
Amis, William Robert, 14, 141
As You Like It (Shakespeare), 107
Auden, W. H., 114, 115, 117, 118, 120

Bardwell, Hilary Ann, 18
Bergonzi, Bernard, 42, 144, 145
Berkhamsted, 18, 44, 57, 117
Berryman, John, 37
Betjeman, John, 81, 129, 131
Black Papers, 132
Bone, Gavin, 15
Braine, John, 149

Cambridge, 15, 21, 22, 23, 72, 74
"Caton, L. S.", 18, 29, 34, 65, 149
City of London School, 15, 79
Conquest, Robert, 118, 132

Crome Yellow (Aldous Huxley), 35
Crysalids, The (John Wyndham), 89

Davie, Donald, 13, 14, 21, 114, 118, 123
Death of the Heart, The (Elizabeth
  Bowen), 81
Deighton, Len, 65, 66
Denmark Hill, 14
Douglas, Keith, 114
Douglas, Norman, 52
"Dover Beach" (Matthew Arnold), 66

Education Act (1944), 23, 24
Eliot, T. S., 71, 142
Enright, D. J., 128

Fielding, Henry, 52, 53
Finnegans Wake (James Joyce), 51
Firbank, Ronald, 84
Forster, E. M., 20, 30, 49, 150
Fothergill, John, 72
Fraser, G. S., 120
Frayn, Michael, 54
"Friends Beyond" (Thomas Hardy), 131

Go-Between, The (L. P. Hartley), 82
Golding, William, 150
Good Food Guide, The, 72
Graves, Robert, 20, 22, 52, 114, 118,
  120, 123
Greene, Graham, 18, 33, 57, 69, 111

Howard, Elizabeth Jane, 22, 141
Hurrell, John D., 145
Hurry On Down (John Wain), 18, 24, 34
Huxley, Aldous, 35, 80

Invitation to the Waltz (Rosamond
  Lehmann), 82

James, Clive, 113, 114, 148
James, Henry, 52, 105
James, M. R., 75, 76, 79
Jill (Philip Larkin), 17, 18

Kinsley, James, 18, 19

Larkin, Philip, 13, 14, 16, 17, 25, 26, 43,
  49, 70, 77, 90, 92, 113, 114, 118

Leavis, F. R., 21
Less Deceived, The (Philip Larkin), 16
Levin, Bernard, 72
Lodge, David, 31, 42, 145, 151
Lough, Ernest, 87

Macleod, Norman, 145–46
MacNiece, Louis, 149
Maugham, W. Somerset, 20, 50, 52, 80, 141
Michie, James, 34
Mixed Feelings (John Wain), 19
Moreschi, Alessandro, 83
"Movement, The", 18, 118, 119, 120
Murdoch, Iris, 149, 150
Music of Time, The (Anthony Powell), 94

New Lines, 118, 119
Norbury, 13, 14
North Ship, The (Philip Larkin), 18

Orwell, George, 35, 78
Owen, Wilfred, 115
Oxford, 15, 17, 23, 110, 111, 130

Piers Plowman (Langland), 72
Poets of the 1950's, 119

Powell, Anthony, 113
Powys, John Cowper, 52

Rape of the Lock, The (Alexander Pope), 95
Right Ho, Jeeves (P. G. Wodehouse), 35
Rolfe, Frederick (Baron Corvo), 85
Room at the Top (John Braine), 23, 34
Russell, "Pee Wee", 16, 131

Sayers, Dorothy L., 78
Signals, Royal Corps of, 16
Sillitoe, Alan, 149, 150
Sorrell and Son (Warwick Deeping), 79, 80
Struggles of Albert Woods, The (William Cooper), 34

Taylor, Elizabeth (novelist), 52
Thomas, Dylan, 18, 19, 39, 119
Toynbee, Philip, 113
Trilling, Lionel, 20

Wain, John, 17, 18, 19, 36, 149
Waugh, Evelyn, 57, 62, 70, 141, 149
Wodehouse, P. G., 35, 36, 58

Yeats, W. B., 92, 121